Demosthenes

THE WORLD OF DEMOSTHENES
MID-4TH CENTURY BCE

MACEDON

Axios

Strymon

Pella

Amphipolis

Thas

Pydna

CHALCIDICE

Olynthus

Potidaea

THESSALY

Pherae

Pagasae

Lamia

Pass of Thermopylae

Delphi

Elateia

Amphissa

PHOCIS

Euboea

Chaeronea

BOEOTIA

Thebes

Ionian Sea

Piraeus

Athens

ATTICA

Corinth

PELOPONNESE

Aegina

Calauria

Troezen

N

W — E

S

Messene

Sparta

Melos

Taenaron

0   100 km

0   100 mi

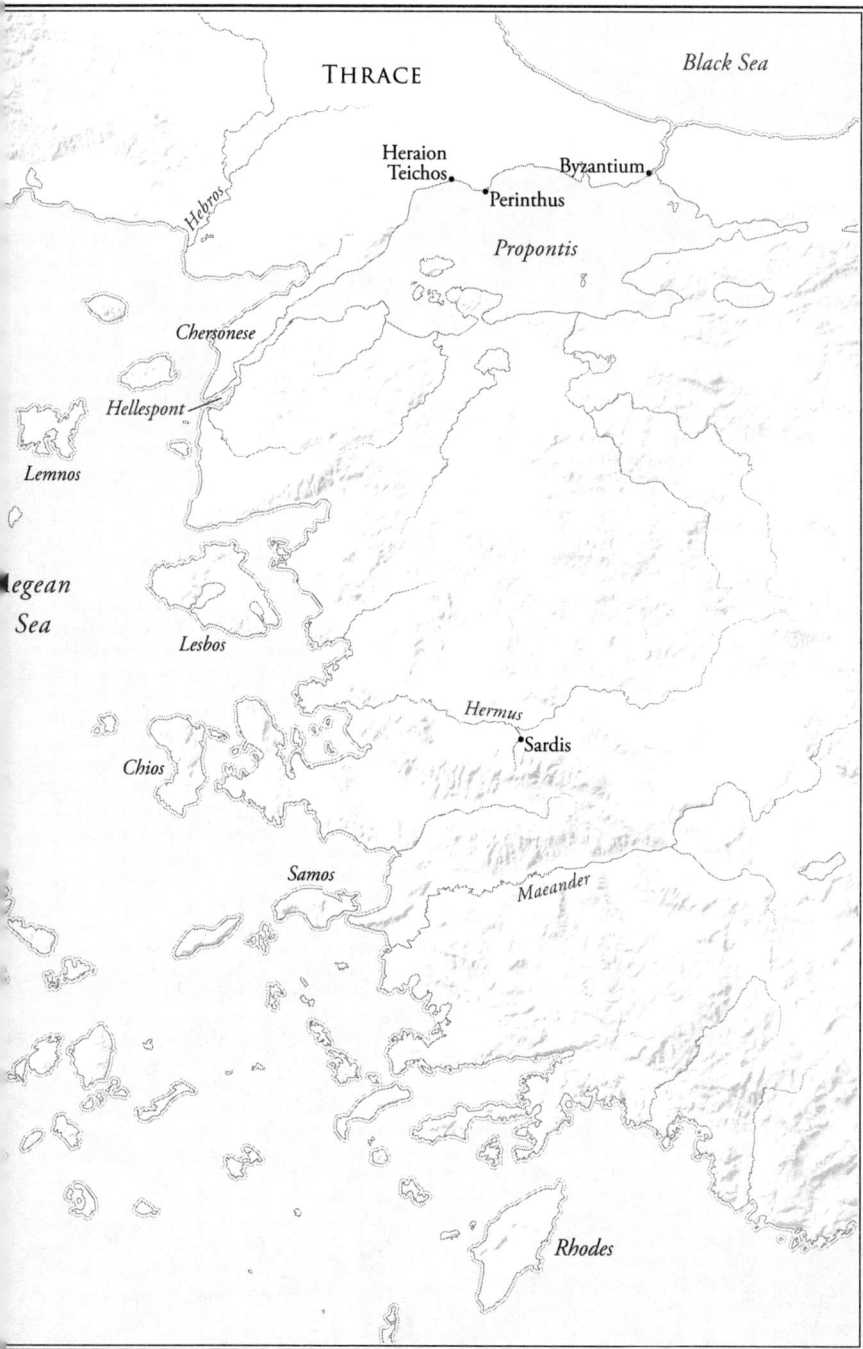

THRACE

Black Sea

Heraion
Teichos
Byzantium
Perinthus

Propontis

Hebros

Chersonese

Hellespont

Lemnos

Aegean
Sea

Lesbos

Hermus
Sardis

Chios

Samos

Maeander

Rhodes

Demosthenes

Democracy's Defender

James Romm

· ANCIENT LIVES ·

Yale
UNIVERSITY PRESS
NEW HAVEN & LONDON

Published with assistance from the foundation established in memory of
Calvin Chapin of the Class of 1788, Yale College.

Frontispiece: Beehive Mapping.

Yale University Press books may be purchased in quantity for
educational, business, or promotional use. For information, please e-mail
sales.press@yale.edu (U.S. office) or sales@yaleup.co.uk (U.K. office).

Set in the eYale typeface designed by Matthew Carter, and Louize,
designed by Matthieu Cortat, by Integrated Publishing Solutions.
Printed in the United States of America.

Library of Congress Control Number: 2024952623
ISBN 978-0-300-26938-3 (hardcover)

A catalogue record for this book is available from the British Library.
Authorized Representative in the EU: Easy Access System Europe,
Mustamäe tee 50, 10621 Tallinn, Estonia, gpsr.requests@easproject.com.

10 9 8 7 6 5 4 3 2 1

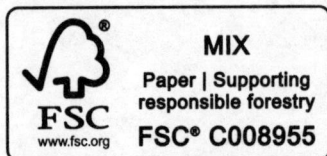

MIX
Paper | Supporting
responsible forestry
FSC
www.fsc.org
FSC® C008955

Contents

Contents

Demosthenes

CHAPTER ONE

I Alone Will Be Shown to Have Spoken the Truth

For the Athenian Assembly, a critical decision was at hand. Two envoys from the Thracian city of Amphipolis, Hierax and Stratocles, had come to Athens to plead for a rescue mission. As they reported from the *bema* — the speaker's platform of the open-air Pnyx, the hillside where the Assembly met — their city was being attacked by Macedon, their neighbor to the west. The defenses of Amphipolis were famously strong, but newly devised siege weapons had been brought against them; without Athenian help in driving the Macedonians back, the walls might easily fail. If they did, no one knew what Philip, the twenty-five-year-old king of Macedon, now mounting his first assault on a major Greek city, was capable of.

No doubt Demosthenes was in the Assembly that day in 357 BCE.[1] Ambitious public figures attended whenever the citizen body met, which happened at least forty times a year, more often in times of crisis. If Demosthenes *was* there, he got his first glimpse, through the envoys' report, of the man with whom he would vie for much of the next two decades, whom he would meet in a high-stakes treaty negotiation, and whose army he would finally confront on the field of battle. Philip was to be his bête noire, his cause célèbre, the springboard of his rise to political fame. Speeches he was soon to deliver from that same bema to that same Assembly would have a single, driving theme, as signaled by the title later given to them, *Philippics* – a word that in English today signifies a scorching verbal attack.

The thousands of Athenians present that day on the Pnyx heard arguments for and against sending help to Amphipolis. In principle, anyone who wished could address the citizen body, the *demos*, in an Assembly meeting, but in practice a few leading citizens dominated debate. These *rhetores*, "public speakers," were comparable to modern-day politicians, although some did not hold, perhaps did not even seek, an elective office. Their goal was to sway the Assembly to their point of view, since from that sway came power, and from power, wealth; bribes, bequests, and favors flowed to those who could tip the scales of opinion. Prominent speakers also attracted like-minded citizens into their orbit, forming what we might think of as transitory, person-centered political parties ("those around X" is a common Greek way to denote a faction, where "X" is the name of a rhetor). Demosthenes would one day control the largest political faction in Athens.

The appeal from the envoys included a startling offer: if the Amphipolitans received Athenian aid against Philip, they would make their city subject to Athens, as it had once been. Amphipolis had in fact been founded by Athens, in 422, and six decades later it represented in Athenian minds the glories of a lost era. Sparta had liberated the city in 404 when it dissolved the Athenian empire, and thereafter Amphipolis had guarded its independence. But now it seemed willing to put its mineral wealth and timber stands back in

Athenian hands. This was an outcome that Athens, still trying to regain its stature half a century after its loss to Sparta, fervently desired.

Aware of how this offer might tempt the Athenians, Philip, while besieging Amphipolis, extended an offer of his own. In a letter he sent to be read aloud in the Assembly, he vowed he would hand Amphipolis over to Athens provided the Athenians gave him a free hand to capture the place. This counteroffer no doubt provoked much debate on the Pnyx. Letting Philip take his objective, then profiting from his success, was by far an easier path than opposing him, but it also meant collaborating with a monarchic, militaristic state and helping a vaguely alien people attack a kindred one. In the eyes of many Greeks, the Macedonians, largely herdsmen and farmers rather than city dwellers, were not true Hellenes, even if their royal family claimed descent from Heracles and thus from Zeus. The idea that Athens might back such a seemingly foreign nation against its own former colonists was troubling, no matter what the reward.

Looming over the Assembly debate was the fact that the power of Athens was stretched very thin. The few Greek states that belonged to its vestigial empire, islands and cities in the eastern Aegean, were on the point of revolt. How many ships could be spared to defend the Amphipolitans, and how quickly could they get to Thrace? Could Athens afford to open a front in the north with so little revenue coming in and so many eastern commitments?

At last it was time for the vote. In the system by which Athens was governed, the purest democracy ever created — that is, for those who were citizens, adults, and male — a simple show of hands by the thousands in the Assembly decided all questions of state. In today's world, the equivalent would be if a nation dissolved its legislature and allowed its people to pass or veto laws, establish or break alliances, even declare war, by clicks on the internet. The volatile system left Athens open to demagogy and led to huge policy errors, as demonstrated during the war with Sparta fifty years earlier. Yet even after losing that war and most of its empire, Athens had held on to its Assembly-based constitution while it slowly rebuilt its navy and worked to recover its mastery of the seas.

As hands went up for the vote on Amphipolis, directional winds decided the question. Philip had cleverly launched his attack during the Etesians, northerlies that blew for several weeks every summer. Athenians did not have the time, or perhaps the will, to send ships into those headwinds; they would not dispatch any aid. Philip's siege of Amphipolis went on undisturbed, his troops assaulting the walls in relays, attacking both day and night. It was not long before the battering rams punched a hole, and the men poured in, butchering those who tried to stand against them. The place that Athenians longed to possess was in Philip's hands and would soon be transferred to theirs — or so they expected.

But that expectation was born of naive optimism, a trait that had often led Athenians astray. Not only did Philip refuse to give Athens his prize, he soon attacked *other* Greek cities in his region, including Athenian allies. He easily captured one such ally, Pydna, after a group of "Philippizers" — a word Demosthenes seems to have coined — betrayed their city and opened the gates to him. Athens perhaps had agreed in a secret negotiation to let Philip have Pydna in exchange for the promised handover of Amphipolis; sources mention rumors to that effect. If such a swap *had* been arranged, Philip broke his word once again and ignored it.

Athenians began to realize that Macedon under Philip was a force to be reckoned with. The large and populous kingdom had always been poorly governed and disunited; the Greeks to its south regarded it as a backward place, no threat to *them*. But Philip, in only two years on the throne, had shown unique talent and energy; he had centralized royal power as never before. All statecraft and all state resources were in the hands of one man, a king in title, but in the role he had played to this point a warlord, leading a massive, highly trained army. To fight him, Athenians were now recognizing, would require unity and commitment — two assets that in the past their fractious city had rarely been able to summon.

In the wake of the fall of Pydna, the Assembly at Athens once more considered its options. Things looked far worse than they had just a few months before, in part because the Aegean states that paid Athens tribute had gone into revolt. Funds were stretched thinner than ever, yet a riposte of some kind was essential. Again by a simple, spontaneous show of hands, the Assembly declared war on Philip. The "war for Amphipolis," as the Athenians hopefully termed it, was under way.

Philip took little notice. As the autumn of 357 set in, with his flag firmly planted in several Greek cities, he marched back to his palace in Pella, the Macedonian royal seat. A new bride awaited him there, his fifth polygamous marriage since taking the throne. He knew he would need to deal with Athens at some point, perhaps appease the people's anger over Amphipolis, but nothing as yet impelled him to do so. Athens lay far to his south, beyond the Thermopylae pass; if he blocked that narrow corridor, no troops could reach him by land, and his nearly landlocked nation was safe from attack by sea.

Soon after Philip's return from the Pydna campaign, his latest wife, Olympias, became pregnant, and in June 356 gave birth to a boy. Philip's son — his second, but soon to become his heir apparent — would one day pose new threats to Athens, to all of Greece, and to Demosthenes in particular. History knows him as Alexander the Great.

———

Demosthenes was in his late twenties when the Amphipolis war was declared, a wealthy, up-and-coming young man with his sights on a speaking career. He had set those sights in his teens, according to Plutarch, his first-century CE biographer, when his tutor took him to observe an important trial. The defendant, Callistratus of Aphidna, one of the leading orators of the day, spoke in his own defense and won over the jury; after his acquittal, jubilant followers showered him with acclaim. Stirred by both the masterful speech and the adoring crowd (says Plutarch), young Demosthenes was hooked. From the start, his ambition had sought two very different goals: eloquence on the one hand and, on the other, the high esteem of the demos.[2]

Demosthenes possessed few of the traits that commanded that esteem. He was physically weak, short of stature, and prone to illness; growing up, he declined to take part in the rough-and-tumble athletics that were central to Greek male maturation and military training. Other boys gave him the nickname "Batalus," mocking his speech defect with a multi-layered word that had the primary meaning "stammerer." But "Batalus" also connoted a lack of machismo; a male musician by that name had broken gender boundaries by appearing onstage in women's footwear. In yet another layer of insult, *batalos* was Greek slang for the anus — a meaning that would later be played on in scurrilous rhetorical attacks. With this cruel moniker, then, Demosthenes was bullied in three ways simultaneously.

Demosthenes' personality also did not seem well suited to public life. Anxious, gloomy, and harsh, he made enemies more easily than friends. He was labeled a "water drinker" because he abstained from wine; he avoided the wine-drinking evenings, known as symposiums, that were central to Athenian socialization. (Later in life, when told that Philip had a prodigious capacity for wine, Demosthenes scoffed that this was the attribute of a sponge, not a monarch.) But isolation gave him more time to dedicate to his craft. He became known as a tireless worker of words who wrote well into the night, so much so that his speeches "smelled of the lamp" (as his critics sneered) the next morning.[3]

Demosthenes had been born to a wealthy father, also named Demosthenes, the owner of two manufacturing shops where huge enslaved gangs toiled away, and a savvy investor to boot. As the family's only son, Demosthenes had every hope of being wealthy himself. But his father died when he was seven, leaving the business and property in the care of two adult nephews and an old family friend. If we trust the account Demosthenes later gave, these three executors ignored their instructions, embezzled most of the money, and sold off the family businesses to enrich themselves. When he reached age eighteen, Demosthenes inherited little more than a talent (six thousand drachmas or, roughly, twenty years' wages for an unskilled worker), though his father had once been worth fourteen talents, an amount that might have been doubled during the subsequent decade if managed correctly.

By that time Demosthenes had set himself to mastering the art of speechwriting, which meant, in a sense, pursuing a legal career. The Athenian court system relied on well-written speeches in a way that far transcends any modern judiciaries. Courts had no judges; huge, randomly chosen juries, numbering in the hundreds or even more than a thousand, decided cases by majority vote immediately upon hearing the speeches given by both sides. Jurors did not deliberate before voting by secret ballot, and forensic evidence was thin or nonexistent; hence an eloquent speech that played on emotion, arousing pity for the accused or anger against him, and that kept the jury engaged with impressive arrangements of words, could go a long way toward winning a case. Both sides in a legal dispute might thus hire speechwriters, *logographoi,* to draft their hours-long pleas.

Demosthenes made up his mind to become a logographos. He is said to have sought out a mentor named Isaeus, who'd had good success at this trade, to instruct him in how to write winning forensic addresses. In addition to needing a source of income, he had his own ax to grind. He was old enough to file lawsuits now, and his sights were set on the three guardians who had purloined his father's estate. He planned to bring them to trial and use his own speechwriting skills to recover his patrimony.

His first legal sally was launched in 364. Demosthenes, then twenty years old, delivered the prosecutorial speech now known as "Against Aphobus 1" (the "1" denotes that it forms the first of a series). In this speech we have the earliest surviving words of the hundreds of thousands Demosthenes would write and declaim in the course of the next four decades.

Aphobus, Demosthenes' cousin, seems to have been the ringleader of the three crooked guardians. Demosthenes attacks him by giving a precise account of all the moneys purloined and squandered, the goods sold off, and the profits skimmed. His ledger-book approach makes for dry reading today, but amid the facts and figures are flashes of verbal brilliance. Take, for example, a passage in which he uses a rhetorical question to launch a barrage of charges, rattles them off in a quickening cadence, then comes back around, with the air of one who has made refutation impossible, to the opening question:

> How could someone prove more clearly that this man has plundered
> everything and spared not even trifles than by using *this* kind of proof,
> along with so many witnesses and testimonials — namely, that he ad-

mitted taking the dowry money and wrote to the executors that he had it; that he took profits out of the factory and didn't show any report; that he sold some of our assets and didn't pass on the proceeds, while other assets he kept for himself and hid them away out of sight; that even on the accounting he himself has turned over, he's stolen such great sums; that on top of all that he concealed the will, he sold all the slaves, he managed everything in a way that not even my worst enemies would do? I don't see how anyone could prove the matter more clearly.[4]

With grandiloquent sentences like these, and accusations that obscured by their number the lack of evidence behind them, Demosthenes swayed the jury and won his case. But Aphobus, in a pattern we might recognize today, used legal maneuvers to escape the court's judgment and avoid repayment.

The trials and proceedings multiplied. Demosthenes struggled for years against his recalcitrant cousins, always winning his cases but never, apparently, getting back much of the money. Meanwhile, he was gaining skill at his newfound trade.

Demosthenes could have sought other mentors besides Isaeus during his formative years. Plato was then leading a new institution in Athens called the Academy, where ambitious, wealthy young men came to learn. One obscure source, impossible to verify, claims that Demosthenes studied with Plato, but neither man mentions the other in any surviving writings.[5] In terms of their intellects and modes of thought, the two had little in common: Demosthenes was nose-to-the-ground and pragmatic, whereas Plato preferred to think in ideals and abstractions. Politically, too, they were worlds apart. Plato thought that assembly-based democracy had failed and needed to be replaced; Demosthenes, though he often railed at the demos for its mistakes or inaction, never questioned the system that gave it executive power. He came to regard himself as that system's best hope of survival, and its survival as the best hope for the Greeks.

Another thinker who was losing patience with democracy, a man named Isocrates, was also teaching in Athens during Demosthenes' youth, training aspiring leaders in the art of public speaking. We hear vague rumors that he too mentored Demosthenes, but there are reasons not to trust these reports.[6] Isocrates, disillusioned by decades of Greek infighting, sought unity and redemption through a single, all-powerful leader, regardless of the cost to political freedom. In the 360s, just as Demosthenes came of age, Isocrates started writing open letters to promising strongmen, something he continued to do throughout the next three decades. Eventually he lit on Philip of Macedon as the hoped-for redeemer of Greece – the very man whom Demosthenes came to regard as Greece's greatest threat. Whatever the two orators had in common professionally, they ended up in opposing camps regarding relations with Philip.

Having launched his career with the Aphobus trials, Demosthenes next looked to speak before the Assembly, where stakes were higher and audiences much larger (perhaps ten thousand or more on some occasions). With his weak chest, he had trouble projecting his voice, and the stammer that led to his nickname drew laughter from those who heard his first public efforts. To build up his lungs, Plutarch says, Demosthenes would recite while climbing hills, jogging, or standing on a beach and shouting above the roar of the waves; to clear up his stutter, he delivered orations with pebbles in his mouth. And since rhetoricians need body language to highlight chief points, Demosthenes rehearsed in front of a full-length mirror. His single-mindedness astonished his peers and generated wild stories. Some said he had built an underground room in which he sequestered himself for months at a time; others, that he had shaved off hair from one-half of his head so that he would look too silly to leave his house. Still others said that, to eliminate an unappealing habit of rolling his shoulder, he had fixed a sword in the wall that would stab him if he moved his arm the wrong way.[7] In the end it was neither teachers nor exercises nor singleminded devotion but rather, according to Plutarch, the advice of an actor named Satyrus that led to a breakthrough. This man had heard Demosthenes speak in public and noted the poor response of his listeners. Satyrus followed the orator home from one such outing and found him disconsolate over his lack of success. He made Demosthenes read out a speech from Greek tragedy; the words came out flat and lifeless. Then Satyrus delivered the speech himself, using the skills of the stage to bring it to life. Demosthenes suddenly realized that writing eloquent speeches was only half the job; when he delivered them, he had to employ a dramatist's toolkit of tone, inflection, and movement. From that point forward, his talent began to blossom.[8]

The Satyrus story related by Plutarch may well be spurious, but it reveals a larger point, one Plutarch often adverts to. Democratic politics in the Greek world (as in our own) included a large measure of theater. When the drama turned turbid and dire, as in a tragic play, it became especially compelling to its "audience," the citizen body. Demosthenes lived in a time when the direst drama of all, a threat to existence itself, would play out among the cities of central Greece, especially Athens and Thebes. He was destined to take on that drama's leading role, although in the eyes of his critics (both ancient and modern) he was badly miscast.

Exactly when Demosthenes moved up from logographos, writer of courtroom speeches, to rhetor, Assembly speaker, is not clear. His earliest extant Assembly speech, "On the Naval Boards," was delivered in 354, when he was thirty years old, but others that have been lost may have preceded it. If that speech *was* his Assembly debut, he certainly made it a striking one. The question before the demos was nothing less than war with the Great King of Persia, Artaxerxes III. The Persians, rulers of Asia, had stayed out of mainland Greece for more than a century by this time, but the King had built up his navy in a way that signaled to some that he meant to invade, as his predecessors Darius and Xerxes had done. Athens had played a huge part in defeating those earlier incursions, in battles that by Demosthenes' day were the stuff of legend. War hawks in Athens longed to lead a crusade once again against a "barbarian" host.

But Athens had changed since those heady days when it had beaten the Persians at Marathon and Salamis. The naval empire that had filled its coffers with tribute had been lost, then partly regained, then lost once more at the same time that the Persian threat seemed to return. Athenians had suffered reverses as first Sparta, then Thebes, became leaders of mainland Greece – the hegemonic role that had once been theirs. Demosthenes lived in diminished times; he knew that fighting the Great King was beyond his city's means. He urged the Assembly not to seek war with Artaxerxes since it was not yet clear whether Persia presented a threat (in fact, the new Persian fleet was aimed at Egypt, not Greece). But that was not the limit of his advice. His larger purpose in the speech, it emerged, was overhaul of the Athenian navy.

Most of the power that Athens still had in the mid-fourth century came from its navy. Its fortified harbor, Piraeus, was the best naval base in Greece, and its populace was expert at building and rowing triremes (the standard warship of the classical age). But triremes were expensive weapons. Their crews of two hundred were paid a daily wage, and their tackle and gear had to be replaced or serviced often. These costs were not subsidized by the state, as with a modern navy, but by wealthy private citizens who took turns serving as trierarch, a post in which they paid the costs of the ships, and might also serve on their decks, for a set span of time. Not all who could afford the expense undertook it. Many shirked by hiding their wealth, and this weakened the fleet.

Demosthenes had, in his youth, served two stints as trierarch, the first time not voluntarily. At age twenty his embezzling cousins pressured him into taking the post by way of a legal maneuver; he managed to scrape together the sum of money he needed only by mortgaging his house. Sometime later, after his legal career had given him more ample means, he became trierarch once again, this time with such success that the city awarded him a prize – an honorary gold crown. His rival trierarchs contested that prize, but Demosthenes proved to a jury's satisfaction that he deserved it. His outraged defense of the excellence of his service, a speech titled "On the Trierarchic Crown," survives.

In the early 350s, after Demosthenes' two tours of duty, Athens replaced the trierarch system with boards of sixty citizens who pooled their money to fund a squadron of ships. The idea was that board members would police one another, since any shortfall by shirkers would have to be made up by others within the pool. Even so, the system had loopholes. Demosthenes perceived that if the boards were smaller, twelve people rather than sixty, they would be more effective at keeping their members honest; the members would also feel more committed to their ships if they were assigned to maintain only three. So in his "On the Naval Boards" speech, after urging the Assembly to avoid war with Persia, he launched into a detailed plan for reform of a system that had been in place only four years.

It took gumption for a political rookie to present such a case, since doing so implied that his elders had erred when designing the boards. But Demosthenes put a bold foot forward in "On the Naval Boards," asserting his right to speak up. "I know that I'm about to say something surprising, but nevertheless it shall be said," he told the Assembly. "I'm confident that if someone examines things rightly, I alone will be shown to have spoken the truth and described what is going to happen." Tall words from a thirty-year-old, perhaps in his first time on the bema, but Demosthenes was presenting big ideas. He pressed for downsized boards, a tighter link between boards and ships, and a list of other reforms, all designed to strengthen the fleet and improve its funding. Then, with his program laid out, he turned back to the question of war against the Great King. If the demos stayed at peace with Artaxerxes, he closed, "you'll do right both by yourselves and by those who gave you the opposite counsel to mine, since you won't be angry at them later for your present mistakes."[9]

The speech was a partial success; the demos voted against the war but did not endorse the reform of the naval system. Recalling this mixed outcome several years later, Demosthenes focused on the antiwar vote and claimed it as a personal victory, won without help from others. "I think some of you remember," he told the Assembly on that later occasion, "when I advised you about the Great King; I was the first to come forward with advice, alone as I think, or perhaps there was one other speaker."[10] Since he was prone to magnifying his achievements (like all politicians), we may doubt he was in such a tiny minority. But he *did* have cause to be proud. On a crucial question of peace or war, he had helped tilt the scales of opinion toward peace. He had made himself a foreign policy voice.

Though war with Artaxerxes had been averted, the conflict with Philip, the war for Amphipolis, went on. Philip continued besieging and capturing Greek cities along his southern borders; when Athens sent ships to defend one of these, they arrived too late. Demosthenes had pointed out flaws in the Athenian naval system, but its biggest flaw was one he could not address. All moves by the fleet had to be debated in the Assembly, then voted on, before the crews could be assembled and ships made ready to sail. The process was toilsome and slow, encumbered by democratic complexities, and unable to keep pace with a dynamic commander like Philip.

In one of the cities he captured by siege, Potidaea, Philip took a group of Athenian settlers prisoner. He did not sell these captives as slaves, as he did in many other cases. He let them return to Athens, unharmed and unransomed — a sign he was seeking a rapprochement. Perhaps, he must have reasoned, if he acted magnanimously, the Philippizers at Athens would gain the upper hand, end the war for Amphipolis, and bring the city over to his side. If the Greek world's greatest navy, that of the Athenians, joined forces with its most powerful army and siege train, his own, they would create an unstoppable combination — one that might conquer the world.

A man whose name he perhaps did not yet know, Demosthenes, would soon make sure that none of those things ever happened.

CHAPTER TWO

That Was the Critical Moment

I n the age of Demosthenes the balance of power in Greece had
become volatile and unstable. A "three-headed monster," as
some wags termed it, dominated the mainland: Athens, Sparta,
and Thebes competed for lead position, forming or breaking alliances with one another as circumstances dictated, trying to bring
smaller states into line with their interests. In 362, when Demosthenes was in his early twenties, Thebes and its allies confronted a
Spartan-Athenian axis in a major showdown, and it seemed that
the outcome would lead to a settled order. But the Battle of Man-
tinea, as it is known, had no clear victor, and the condition of Hellas
remained as confused as ever.

As the armies disengaged and went home, the cities of Greece —
all except Sparta, determined to pursue its own goals — agreed to
each keep what it had, that is, to accept the status quo and halt the
interstate violence. In Greek terms such a blanket treaty was known
as a Common Peace. Several such pacts had been tried earlier but
had not endured for long, since few states could pass up the temp-
tation to break them. After 362 it was Athens that threatened the

Peace, by using its fleet to control and tax other Greeks. Conservatives like Isocrates urged Athens to rein itself in and live within its means. Keeping an empire that spanned the Aegean was terribly costly, Isocrates wrote in "On the Peace," and making subjects pay that cost turned friends into enemies. Indeed, several large states rebelled against Athens in 357, as we have seen, launching what became known as the Social War. After two years of struggle Athens was forced to grant their autonomy, unable to afford the cost of suppression.

Demosthenes' effort at naval-funding reform, in his speech "On the Naval Boards," was one of several ideas brought forward at this time for improving finances. If Athens were to regain Amphipolis or maintain control of the seas, it had to find ways to raise money other than shaking down other Greeks. A different scheme was put forward by Xenophon, a former student of Socrates', who was ending his storied career at the time Demosthenes was beginning his. In his last known work, *Revenues,* Xenophon advised the Athenians to buy up slaves and use them to better exploit the silver mines south of their city. His proposals, like those of Demosthenes, went unheeded. Meanwhile, Athenian revenues reportedly shrank to 130 talents of silver per year, less than a quarter of what the city had taken in at the height of its power.[1]

Among those grappling with this shortfall was a man named Eubulus, who rose to prominence in the mid-350s. As manager of the Theoric Fund, a pool of public money reserved for domestic use, Eubulus showed great acumen and thus gained a leading voice in public affairs. He used his sway to advocate against military adventures that drained the state's treasuries. The fleet and the army should only be used, he argued, against threats to the city itself, not to its overseas interests. At the time he came on the scene, such direct threats had not yet emerged, but this would soon change.

Other cities of Greece were also short of resources in the 350s and in need of ways to raise cash. A Spartan king, Agesilaus, died in Egypt in 358, fighting for pay (at age eighty-six!) to help provide funds for Sparta. Thebes, in decline after losing its two greatest leaders, exported a corps of five thousand soldiers across the Aegean to aid a rebellious Persian satrap. A ruler of Thessaly, Alexander of Pherae, who employed an expensive mercenary army, ordered a lightning raid by sea on the Athenian harbor, Piraeus; his crews went ashore, grabbed sackfuls of coin from the currency traders who worked there, then dashed back to their ships and sailed home. It was, in effect, the world's first recorded bank robbery.

The greatest and boldest cash grab of all, however, was one carried out by the people of Phocis, the region of northwest Greece that bordered on Delphi. Their actions in 356 were to have profound consequences for both Athens and Demosthenes, as well as for Philip of Macedon, over the decade that followed – a decade defined by what is now known as the Third Sacred War.

The shrine of Delphi, the seat of Apollo's most trusted oracle, was by this time a storehouse of wealth. Petitioners who had received a favorable reply to a question, who sought one, or who wanted to put their piety on display had made dedications, often of silver and gold, over the course of centuries. The sanctity of the shrine had always protected its treasures, but that penumbra had begun to wear thin. In 356 the Phocians, their livelihood threatened by a decree of the Amphictyony – Delphi's governing board – sent an armed force, made up largely of mercenaries, and took over the shrine. Promising to replace what they used, they began to plunder the precious metals stored there and melt them down into coin; the money they gained went to hire more soldiers and strengthen their position as occupiers.

The Amphictyonic board, made up of representatives from twelve cities but dominated by Thebes, called on the Greeks to go to war on behalf of the shrine. (This was the third time in its history the board had done so, hence the name Third Sacred War.) Their call forced many states, especially Athens, to weigh the moral duty of rescuing Delphi against how the war would affect the balance of power. Since Thebes was leading the fight against Phocis, Athens and Sparta lined up on the opposite side; both were concerned that Thebes was becoming too strong. Besides, Athens had a long-standing alliance with Phocis, as well as a more recent one with Sparta, its old enemy now become its friend.

The Sacred War also heightened an internal conflict in Thessaly, the large and populous realm that stood between the southern Greek cities and Macedon farther north. With their powerful cavalry and control of the pass of Thermopylae, the best route south into central Greece, the Thessalians could have played a crucial part in the war, but they were themselves divided. A tyrannical clan who controlled the city of Pherae, in Thessaly's east, were firmly allied with the Phocians, while the inland regions were staunchly opposed to that clan and to the Phocians as well. These internal tensions grew worse in 354, when the western Thessalians called in Philip of Macedon, their powerful neighbor, and made him their archon, essentially their commander-in-chief. The Pherae faction responded by calling on Phocis (or, rather, the huge hired army fighting on Phocis's behalf).

Athens watched nervously as these realignments took place and as Philip, by entering Thessaly, moved a giant step southward. Thessaly was physically separated from central Greece by rugged mountains; through them, the pass of Thermopylae provided only a narrow path, easily closed. But Philip's presence in Thessaly was nonetheless worrisome, for it suggested he might get involved in the stalemated Sacred War. Thebes had won an initial victory but failed to follow it up, and the Phocians, drawing on Delphi's vast treasure, had made good their losses by hiring more mercenaries. Their army became something new to the Greeks: an assemblage of rootless, stateless men fighting only for pay, not for a national cause. Yet Athens had taken this army's side against all who sought to dislodge it, and that decision, as now appeared, might bring on a new clash with Philip.

Eastern Thessaly soon became a major theater of war, as Philip arrived to dislodge the Pherae tyrants and the Phocians moved in to support them. The tough Phocian fighters, under the command of a warlord named Onomarchus, won an initial engagement in 354, but both sides returned for a rematch the following year. This time Athens took a hand in the struggle. The Assembly voted to send a fleet north to rendezvous with the Phocians near Pagasae, the harbor of Pherae, which Philip's army had put under siege.

No speeches from that Assembly meeting survive, so we do not know how Demosthenes viewed the conflict. Later he would up-braid the Athenians for acting too slowly at Pagasae, as they had done previously at Pydna and other places. "If we'd come to the aid of any of these from the first with zeal as the situation required, we would today be dealing with a weaker, more tractable Philip," he admonished his compatriots four years later with benefit of hind-sight.[2] In truth it was hard for a fleet controlled by assembly to counter a warrior-monarch who simply gave marching orders, and whose forces were also far closer to the combat zone.

For Athens, Pagasae turned out to be the worst case yet of ar-riving too late. As the Athenian fleet approached the Thessalian shore, the commander, Chares, saw desperate men in the water trying to swim to his ships. The battle was in full swing, and the Phocians were losing. Philip was using small catapults to bombard them with stones, the first recorded deployment in Greece of field artillery weapons. The Phocian line was broken and in full flight, with Macedonian cavalry slashing them down as they fled. Of twenty thousand Phocian troops, six thousand were killed that day, including Onomarchus – a staggering casualty rate for the time. Another three thousand were taken prisoner. The Phocians' strength had been cut nearly in half in one day. There was little for Chares to do but sail home and deliver the news. Athens had failed once again to help an ally in need.

In his management of this battle, Philip tried to appear not as an aggressor but as a pious defender of Delphi. He sent his troops into combat wearing laurel sprigs on their helmets, a symbol of Delphic Apollo. When the battle was over he meted out punishment to his prisoners as befit temple robbers. Instead of selling them into slavery, he herded all three thousand troops into the sea to be drowned by the incoming tide. Their bodies could thus not be recovered for burial or cremation by their kin. As for Onomarchus, who was dead before the battle ended (probably killed by his own disillusioned troops), Philip nailed his corpse to a stake to rot.

This stunning victory at the Battle of Crocus Field gave Philip new options and caused deep concern in Athens. With the tyrants of Pherae uprooted – they were granted safe passage to leave the region – all Thessaly lay open to Philip, right up to the pass of Thermopylae. He might, if he chose, try to transit that pass in pursuit of the Phocians; once through, who knew where he might turn? If he came into central Greece, he would pose a direct threat to Athens.

For once, Athens acted with speed. Eubulus, in charge of the city's finances, opened his tightly guarded coffers and allotted two hundred talents for soldiers and ships. He had argued against such an expenditure unless Athens itself was at stake; now it seemed the condition was being met.

As they headed toward the south end of Thermopylae, the troops sent by Athens were no doubt in mind of a similar mission conducted many years previously. In 480 BCE, Greek infantrymen had gone to Thermopylae to stop a different land army, the Persians, from coming through. After holding back the invaders for several days, nearly three hundred Spartans had died in the pass, an episode enshrined in Greek lore as a noble sacrifice (and commemorated in the modern *300* graphic novel and film). Thermopylae, the site of the Spartan mass grave, had come to stand as a symbol of Greek defiance in the face of "barbarian" hordes. But the new defense of the pass by Athens was less sharply defined. Though some insisted that Philip too belonged to an alien race, others were less certain. Ten years earlier, Philip had sponsored competitors in the Olympic games, a privilege open only to Greeks, and one of his racing horses had come in first. The coinage he issued soon afterward, displaying a horse and rider, proclaimed his place in the circle of Hellenism.

Whether Greek or non-Greek, Philip would pose a direct threat to Athens if he got through the pass. With its dispatch of troops, the Assembly showed it would not allow this to happen. Philip took the point: when he reached the top of the pass and found that the bottom was guarded, he turned his army around and withdrew without forcing the issue.

For the first time in years, Athens had put a check on the power of Macedon. Despite all the times they had come up short, all the allies they had lost, all the occasions they had arrived too late, the Athenians still had the means to keep Philip at bay — for the moment.

Demosthenes had as yet, as far as we know, paid little attention to Philip. He mentioned him briefly in "On the Rhodians' Freedom," delivered in 353 or shortly thereafter.[3] In that speech Demosthenes had used Philip as an example of a ruler who caused little worry at

Athens, in contrast to the Persian Great King, who caused much. "I often see some of you slighting Philip as a person of little concern, but fearing the King as a mighty enemy," he told the Assembly on that occasion.[4] Though clearly he distanced himself from this view, he said nothing more about why he considered it wrong.

"On the Rhodians' Freedom" addresses a policy choice that in Demosthenes' eyes had ideological meaning. The island of Rhodes had been part of the Athenian naval empire until the Social War broke up the league. The newly free Rhodians, under pressure from Persia, changed their constitution from democratic to oligarchic and exiled the leaders of the former regime. Those exiles had come to Athens seeking help in taking back power. They requested Athenian ships to help them drive out the oligarchs and make Rhodes democratic once more. For Athens to do this meant risking a clash with Artaxerxes, the Persian Great King, who far preferred that Aegean states stay under control of his puppets. But in "On the Rhodians' Freedom," Demosthenes argued, in words that echo today, that Athens had to stand up for fellow democracies.

"You've fought many wars, Athenians, against both democracies and oligarchies," Demosthenes told the Assembly; but those wars were different from one another. Fights with democracies, he said, involve land disputes, or competition for leadership of Greece; those with oligarchies are, more vitally, "for the sake of a form of government and for the sake of freedom." Demosthenes argued that fellow democracies pose less of a threat, so it was in the Athenians' interest to support them. He illustrated the point with a surprising assertion. "I don't shrink from saying that I think you'd do better to have *all* the Greeks democratic, and at war with you, than for them *all* to be oligarchies and your allies. For I think you'd easily make peace with those who are free, whenever you chose to, but your friendship with oligarchies would never be secure."[5]

Just as the spread of democracy helped ensure safety, Demosthenes pointed out, the spread of oligarchy spelled danger. "They [the oligarchs] know that you alone will restore freedom; and the source from which they expect trouble to arise for themselves, they will want to destroy."[6] In this way he portrayed the proposed mission to Rhodes, and the defense of democracy generally, as both self-protection for Athens and a moral crusade.

Athenians tended to frame foreign policy choices in terms of the tension between self-interest and what was morally right. Thucydides, in his so-called Melian dialogue, put these two terms into stark opposition at a moment when Athens, in pursuit of empire, was set to besiege the neutral island of Melos. He depicted the Melians appealing to the gods in the name of justice, even as the Athenians mocked them as pious fools. Yet we cannot say that Thucydides thought the Athenians wrong, even when they later destroyed and recolonized Melos. The world, after all, was a dangerous place, and naked self-interest was sometimes the wisest course.

Demosthenes, in "For the Rhodians' Freedom," tried to bring self-interest and justice, the poles of Thucydidean thought, into alignment. Supporting democracy at Rhodes was morally right *and* advantageous, he argued — a seemingly irresistible combination. He laid out a grand, sweeping mission for Athens: to advance the cause of democracy throughout Hellas and thereby safeguard the chief democratic state.

Doubtless the speakers supporting the other side were partisans of Eubulus, the high priest of fiscal restraint. Athens could not afford a Rhodian adventure, those orators no doubt argued; it had to conserve resources to meet direct threats. In "For the Rhodians' Freedom" Demosthenes gave no quarter to these opponents, depicting them as traitors to Athens, crooks on the payroll of foreign powers, and cowards who had deserted their duty and ought to lose their citizen rights. All the same, his opponents prevailed. The Assembly brushed Demosthenes' speech aside and declined to send forces to Rhodes.

In his first few years of speaking before the Assembly, Demosthenes had enjoyed precious little success. He had helped make the case (an easy one) against war with Persia but failed to get his naval reforms enacted or win support for the Rhodian democrats. In another early outing, the speech "For the Megalopolitans" (probably from 352), he lost again, unsuccessfully urging Athenians to loosen ties with the Spartans by aiding one of Sparta's adversaries. That move, too, would have entailed a commitment of forces to places where many in the Assembly, especially Eubulus, did not think they belonged. The "Athens First" party, if we may call it that, had held sway during all those debates, convincing a majority of the demos.

To start winning Assembly votes, it seemed Demosthenes had to show that the very existence of Athens, not merely its interests, was threatened. Philip of Macedon was about to help him make that stronger case.

The attempt by Philip to march through the Thermopylae pass had alarmed the Athenians, but his moves the following year, toward the straits of Hellespont (modern Dardanelles), alarmed them far more. Shipments of grain from Black Sea ports came through these straits, and if they were stopped, as Sparta had done in the previous century, Athens would starve. Hence in 351, when Philip campaigned into Thrace toward the crucial waterway, it was feared that he meant to apply a chokehold. When he laid siege to a place called Heraion Teichos, on the Sea of Azov, that fear turned to panic.

Athens voted to send an emergency squad of forty triremes, paid for by a special tax levy and crewed by citizen rowers. This meant mobilizing most of the men of military age — twenty-five of the city's forty eligible age groups. Athens was gearing up for a showdown at last. But then news arrived that Philip was ill, perhaps dead, and his siege of Heraion Teichos had been abandoned. The expedition was put on hold and, as ten months went by, allowed to shrink to something more modest, a mere patrol force manned by mercenaries.

In the wake of this downscaling Demosthenes delivered the speech now called the "First Philippic" (these titles are not his own but were devised later). He had seen how swiftly and zealously Athens reacted when its food supply was threatened, and also how quickly its zeal had then dissipated. He aimed in the speech to recover that urgency, overcome his city's complacency and inertia, and persuade the Assembly to send a far larger force than was planned.

He began by explaining why he had taken the bema *first*, before the more senior speakers who usually would have had precedence. He was thirty-three at this time and still a nonentity compared with men like Eubulus and his fellow conservative statesman Phocion. "If in the past these men had given you the advice that was needed, there would be no need now for you to seek advice," Demosthenes opened, striking a typically combative note.[7] The rivalry between Assembly speakers was always hot, and comments were often pugilistic; no points were awarded for tact or good sportsmanship.

Demosthenes tried to shake up Athens by setting off rhetorical fireworks. In a passage later praised by the author of *On the Sublime*, an ancient Greek study of great literary effects, he barraged the Assembly with questions as though cross-examining a defendant:

> When, Athenians, will you do what needs doing? What are you waiting
> for? "When some necessity arises." Then what should the events before
> us be called? For I consider shame over one's situation to be, for free
> men, the greatest necessity. Or tell me, do you want to go around ask-

ing one another, "What news?" Could anything be more urgent news than this: a Macedonian is at war with the Athenians and is controlling the affairs of the Greeks? "Is Philip dead?" "No by Zeus, but he's ill." What's the difference to you? Even if he dies, you'll quickly create a new Philip, if this is the way you attend to your affairs.[8]

Athens, he continued, has thus far only reacted to provocations, and always too late, rather than taking the initiative. He memorably compared his city to a "barbarian" boxer, an untrained hack, who moves his hands to cover the place he was hit rather than raising them to ward off a new blow.[9]

With a list of concrete proposals, Demosthenes outlined a two-pronged strategy. He asked for fifty warships, plus transport for five hundred horses, to confront Philip in Thrace immediately. Another, smaller force, ten ships bearing two thousand infantry and two hundred cavalry, would settle in for a longer stay in that region, with fresh soldiers rotating in at intervals. This smaller force would act as a raiding party, avoiding battle — for Philip would win any clash — but doing what damage it could and drawing Philip away from his primary targets. Among the two thousand infantry, Demosthenes specified, at least five hundred ought to be citizen troops; the rest could be mercenaries. The alternative, as he well knew, might be a force of *nothing but* mercenaries, for Athenians, in his view, had grown too accustomed to paying others to fight.

How were the costs of these squads to be met? Demosthenes described how to raise the required funds, but his proposals are lost. The manuscripts that contain his speech bear a unique rubric, "Apodeixis Porou" (Explanation of Revenue), indicating that a document was read aloud at that point — but the document itself is missing. It is hard to imagine what solutions it might have contained; Athens was badly stretched. Indeed, in proposing the raiding force—which would stay in the field for months, a huge fiscal commitment—Demosthenes had to suggest that the soldiers be given only a *siteresion*, a "meal allowance" of two obols per day, less than half the usual wages. (He anticipated that they would make up the shortfall by pillage.) To those who found this scheme miserly, Demosthenes had a rejoinder: "I am myself prepared to sail with the troops as a volunteer and take what comes."[10] No one, it seems, took him up on that offer.

Reduction of pay was a small concession to Eubulus and his faction, the fiscal conservatives. Even so, the proposals made in the "First Philippic" were wildly expensive, out of step with the strategy of hoarding resources to meet existential threats. Demosthenes might mock this strategy with his lampoon of the amateur boxer who only reacts and never anticipates, but the cash-poor city could not afford to do more. Unlike a modern nation-state that can borrow money in wartime, Athens had to live within its means.

Though later hailed as a revelatory address, the "First Philippic" failed to inspire the demos. Athens voted for a much smaller measure, a fleet of ten "empty" ships—that is, triremes without a full crew—under one Charidemus, a dubious soldier of fortune who had only recently become an Athenian citizen. A bequest of five talents was given to this newcomer to hire more men when he reached the straits; that small amount meant that the new recruits would live, in part, on their pillage (in this at least, Demosthenes got his way). The meager expedition has left no trace in our sources, so it must have accomplished little. Philip kept his gains from the Thracian campaign, though he failed to take Heraion Teichos, perhaps because of his illness.

Looking back on this moment three years later, Demosthenes, in another Assembly speech, reproached Athens for its failure to act. "When word came that Philip was ill or dead (both were reported), you thought the critical moment had passed for sending aid, and dissolved the fleet," he reminded his hearers. "But *that* was the critical moment. If you had sent aid *then* to that region, as we had voted, and done so with zeal, Philip would not be troubling us *now* when he has recovered his health."[11]

Those three intervening years would indeed give Athenians cause to regret that they had acted slowly, or stinted on resources, or — what Demosthenes always most dreaded — not acted at all.

CHAPTER THREE

When Will You Do What
Is Needed, if Not Now?

B y the midpoint of the fourth century, Athens, in Demosthenes' view, had made error after error, passing up chances
to stop Philip's expansion. But given the pace of Philip's campaigns,
more chances were always emerging. Athens had failed to support
the Amphipolitans, even when they had offered the prize of their
city's allegiance, but in 349, eight years later, a new such offer arrived before the Assembly. This one came from Olynthus, the powerful city that headed the League of the Chalcidice.

Olynthus had in the past held aloof from Athens, preferring
to keep the hand-shaped northern peninsula, the Chalcidice, free
from outside interference. It had struck an alliance with Philip in
357, believing Philip's vows that he meant no harm to the league.
But the growing power of Macedon convinced Olynthus to look for
a counterweight. In 352 it began to warm toward Athens, as Philip
began to reveal his designs on the league. By 349 he had already
entered the Chalcidice and taken a few smaller cities when Olynthus, foreseeing it might well be next, sent envoys to Athens in

hopes of a mutual-defense treaty. The Assembly again had choices to make: How thinly could Athens stretch its resources to help a distant ally? How far did the city's essential interests extend?

Demosthenes once again took the bema to urge the Assembly to act with speed and force. In the first of his three "Olynthiacs," Demosthenes outlined a two-pronged approach to defending the Chalcidice, similar to what he had once proposed for Thrace. One force would be sent to defend Olynthus, a second to ravage Philip's coastal possessions. Neither would be effective without the other, Demosthenes argued, for Philip could merely outlast the defending force, unless he had to decamp to deal with the raiders, or he could easily take on the raiders after the fall of an undefended Olynthus. Demosthenes did not suggest specific numbers of ships or troops in this speech, or total up the costs, as he had done in the "First Philippic." It must have been clear to all that the plan was expensive.

As in the "First Philippic," Demosthenes set himself against the Athens First stance that was founded on lack of money. His rejoinder to the Eubulus faction was sharp. "You have money, Athenians; more than anyone else has," he told the Assembly, "but you take it in as you wish to."[1] That last cryptic phrase may well have referred to the Theoric Fund, Eubulus's special preserve, set aside for domestic uses; its name (Spectatorship Fund) was derived from its primary purpose, to subsidize theater attendance at the yearly drama performances. Athenians, with their reverence for plays, had made this fund inviolable, decreeing penalties for anyone who even proposed reapportioning it. In Demosthenes' eyes this meant that the Stratiotic Fund, the military budget, was being starved.

Aware of the legal perils involved, in his "First Olynthiac" Demosthenes tiptoed around the idea of tapping Theoric money. "'What's this?' someone might say; 'Are you proposing we consider these funds military?' By Zeus I am not," he assured the Assembly, carefully steering clear of the demarcation. "But I *do* believe that soldiers must be provided for."[2] If money for soldiers could be raised only by taxes, then let there be taxes. Within a few months, as the plight of Olynthus grew worse, he would become bolder in crossing the fiscal line.

Demosthenes tried to convince the Assembly that Philip presented an existential threat. "By the gods, which of you is so simple-minded as not to recognize that the war over there will come here, if we do not take action?" he demanded.[3] Ignoring the point that Athens could, if it wished, block off the Thermopylae pass, he imagined a dire scenario: Philip in central Greece, teaming up with the Thebans, who had no love for Athens, to mount a combined attack. (Things would nearly play out in this way a decade later, as we shall see.) The cost of *that* war, a fight for survival, would be far higher than any preventive measures Athens might undertake for *this* one.

The Assembly did not adopt Demosthenes' two-pronged proposal, but it did show a will to do *something*. Athens struck an alliance with Olynthus and sent a general, Chares, the former defender of Thrace, to the Chalcidice with two thousand *peltasts*, light-armed infantrymen. The plan was not to bring Philip to battle – that would require more men, with heavier armor – but to limit his movements and make his campaign more costly. What Chares' force accomplished is not known, but it could not have been much, since Philip made steady progress, bringing league cities under his sway one by one. Most of the troops under Chares were mercenaries, lacking the motivation of native Athenians. Demosthenes had made the point in his "First Philippic" that Athens could not rely on such men, and he may have been right.

Some weeks or months later (the timing is uncertain), Demosthenes again addressed the Assembly on the problem of Olynthus. His theme this time was the ease with which a degenerate, drunken, unpopular Philip could be beaten by the Athenians. He claimed to have inside information about Philip's court from an unnamed source "who is unable to lie," and based on that report he painted a picture of debauchery and dysfunction:

> He [the informant] says that if there is any man among them skilled in war and combat, Philip thrusts him aside out of envy, wanting all successes to appear to be his own doing. . . . And if there's any sober or just man who can't stand the dissolute way of life every day, the drunkenness, and the dancing of the *kordax*, such a person is thrust aside and considered a nobody. So those who are left as Philip's coterie are thieves and flatterers and people whose drunken dancing is such as I now shrink from describing to you.[4]

The picture is tinged with suggestions of lurid sex, for the kordax dance was infamous for its lascivious buttock movements. In such ways, using a source that he did not name and who may not have existed, Demosthenes tried to evoke not fear of Philip the king, but utter contempt for Philip the human being.

This second Olynthus speech did not propose any concrete measures. It was meant to shore up morale and assure the Assembly, even if falsely, that Athens had every hope of winning the war. Demosthenes compared Philip's empire to a house built on rotten foundations; Philip's so-called allies, he claimed, mistrusted and feared him, and would desert him as soon as they were offered the chance. Demosthenes swore to his hearers that right—in the sense of just dealings and promise keeping—would triumph over might in the end. "It cannot be — cannot be — Athenians, that a wrongdoer and an oath breaker and a liar acquires a power that's stable; such things endure for an instant or for a short time, and flourish on hopes if fortune favors them, but in time they are laid bare and collapse on themselves."[5] Of course, Athens too had done dirty deeds in the past and had broken faith with allies, but Demosthenes knew the value of putting his city on the moral high ground.

That Philip *had* been favored by fortune, Demosthenes could not deny, but luck, he insisted, could hold out for only so long. More lasting and potent was the favor of the divine, and Demosthenes was convinced that it lay with Athens, not Philip. He opened the speech on this note. "On many occasions, as it seems to me, one can see that the goodwill of the gods belongs to this city," he began, striking a pious tone unusual for his speeches. Later he returned to the point: "I see you have many more opportunities for getting the gods' favor than *that* man has," he averred, referring to Philip.[6] Divine favor, as we have seen, is mocked in Thucydides' Melian dialogue as the last resort of the powerless, but here it is seen as a genuine source of strength. Demosthenes made the case — so often, we know, debunked in history's annals — that justice and decency matter in foreign relations; bad actors would not, *could* not, prevail in the end.

Some weeks or months after the "Second Olynthiac," Philip was still on the attack, this time headed straight for Olynthus. Up to this point Philip had always assured the Olynthians that they were not in danger, hoping to keep them off guard. Even as he marched toward their walls, he kept his intentions cloaked until he was only five miles away. He then sent a message that drew back the veil: either the Olynthians must cease to reside in Olynthus or *he* must cease to reside in Macedon, he threatened. He had already cut the city off from the sea, and thus from food supplies, by capturing its harbor. Olynthus once more appealed to Athens for help, more urgently than before.

Perhaps it was at this juncture (the timing again is unclear) that Demosthenes delivered his "Third Olynthiac," the longest and most emphatic speech of the series. This time he aimed his rhetorical darts not only at Philip but at his own system, assembly-based democracy, and what he described as its love of panderers.

"Ever since speakers came on the scene who ask you, 'What is your wish? What decree shall I write? How can I please you?' the affairs of the city are handed off for the sake of the moment's gratification," Demosthenes charged, using a metaphor from drinking parties — the interests of Athens were "handed off" in the way a cup of wine is passed when the drinker has had his own turn.[7] It was not thus in former times, he averred, when speakers like Pericles held the bema and told the demos what was best rather than what it wanted to hear. Demosthenes aspired to a similar role, for in this speech he urged a measure he knew would be unpopular, if not dangerous to mention. He asked for the untouchable Theoric Fund to be touched.

Just a few months earlier he had shrunk from proposing this change, wary of legal consequences. Now, he could find no other way to mount the strong response that Olynthus required. Aiming his rhetoric squarely at Eubulus, without naming names, Demosthenes characterized the Theoric Fund as one more sop by which politicians curried favor and won adherents. "They lead you into these things and tame you and make you their pet," he told the Assembly, referring to the heads of the fund. Addiction to such handouts had made the demos passive and self-content, for "whatever habits a people have, so must their spirit necessarily be." Only by tapping the fund could Athens muster a force to counter Philip — a move that Demosthenes described, in a series of rapid-fire questions, as urgent.

When will you do what is needed, if not now? Are not all the places *ours* that the fellow has taken? And if he masters *this* place as well

[Olynthus], won't we endure the greatest shame of all men? Aren't the
ones now at war with him the ones whom we promised to readily aid,
if they should go to war? Is he not a foe? Does he not possess what is
ours? Is he not a *barbaros*? Or anything one might call him?[8]

That word *barbaros* lands like a hammer blow. With it, Demosthenes cast Philip as an outsider and cultural inferior. The Macedonian
royals claimed that their ancestors hailed from the city of Argos, in
the Peloponnese, but no one quite knew how Hellenic they were;
the question was spun different ways for different agendas. This
was not the first time, nor the last, that Demosthenes made clear
what side of that fence he was on.

Demosthenes conceded in the "Third Olynthiac" that his words
would be unpleasant to hear, though he hoped he would not be
hated for speaking them. Nonetheless there were those in the city
who *did* hate him, perhaps because of that speech. In an incident
that took place in the spring of 348, shortly after the speech was
delivered, a certain Meidias, a friend of Eubulus, showed his dis-
dain for the brash upstart who had dared to propose making use
of the sanctified fund. We have only Demosthenes' account of the
episode — doubtless one-sided, since it was part of a prosecutorial
speech, but nonetheless fascinating for its picture of the polemical
tone of Athenian public life. Let us take a brief look at this clash,
while the fate of besieged Olynthus hangs in the balance.

Meidias was a wealthy man with political connections at the high-
est level, including to Eubulus. He was also apparently friends with
one of Demosthenes' crooked guardians and took a hand on behalf
of those men in the estate disputes. Suddenly, in 348, after more
than a decade without recorded flare-ups, his dislike of Demosthenes escalated into open warfare. It is reasonable to suppose that the

"Third Olynthiac," delivered a month or two earlier, had reignited the old antipathy.

During that intervening time a new foreign policy crisis had erupted, again putting Demosthenes (by his own account) on the opposite side from Eubulus. A pro-Philip faction had arisen in Euboea, an island that Athens considered a vital and reliable ally, and a ruler there requested Athenian help in suppressing it. Eubulus supported the intervention, but Demosthenes opposed it—alone among those who took the bema, he later claimed—because he wanted all his city's resources sent to the Chalcidice. Eubulus carried the vote, and a large force was sent to Euboea, including both Demosthenes and Meidias in the ranks of the soldiers. The campaign became a debacle when the ruler who had called the troops in changed sides and went over to Philip. Thousands of Athenians were taken prisoner and had to be ransomed back at huge expense. Euboea, which lay just off Attica's shores, was lost to the Athenian sphere of influence (though Athens would later regain it by ousting the Philippizers).

Before he left for Euboea, Demosthenes had taken on the position of *choregos*, a post in which he financed a choral performance combining poetry, music, and dance. To serve in this role was a civic honor, especially if the chorus one sponsored at the yearly festival of Dionysus received first prize from a panel of judges. Demosthenes, by a special exemption granted to choregoi, came back from the Euboea campaign to prepare his performance, and Meidias returned soon afterward. Back in Athens, Meidias undertook to sabotage the upcoming show.

He started by blocking Demosthenes from hiring his choice of dancers, opposing exemptions that would have let talented young men avoid the Euboea campaign. Then he organized a break-in at the costume shop where Demosthenes was having gold crowns and elaborate costumes fashioned for his dancers. The goal was to destroy the gear, but apparently it did not succeed. Meidias also suborned the choral director whom Demosthenes had hired and persuaded him to quit the production; luckily, a talented flutist, Telephanes, stepped in.

Finally the day of performance arrived, and the dancers were set to make their entrance into the Theater of Dionysus. At the crucial moment, they found that Meidias had nailed shut the *paraskenia,* the chambers through which they must pass to get into the dance space; they had to make their way by a less impressive route. In any case their efforts were doomed from the start, for Meidias had bullied the judges and rigged the contest against them. Meidias ended the day by picking a fight with Demosthenes, who was seated among the crowd near the front of the theater, and punching him in the face in front of the gathered thousands.

What could have prompted this public display of ill-will? Demosthenes did not speculate on his assailant's motives in the speech with which he brought suit two years later, "Against Meidias." But he clearly was getting under the skin of the Eubulus faction, the circle to which Meidias belonged. Eubulus himself was present at the trial brought on by that suit, as we know from "Against Meidias." He had intended to speak on Meidias's behalf and influence others to do so, but Demosthenes called him out in the speech in order to warn him off: "If you want to wrong me, Eubulus," he proclaimed to the open court, " – but by the gods I don't know what you're paying me back for – . . . take whatever lawful penalty you wish from me, but don't take away the recompense I'm due for this illegal act of hubris committed against me!"⁹

We do not know how Demosthenes' case against Meidias was resolved. We do hear that Demosthenes settled the suit for a sum of three thousand drachmas, but that report comes from another political rival, Aeschines (whom we shall soon meet more fully). In the speech "Against Meidias," however, Demosthenes claimed that he would never accept a settlement, since the wrongs done to him demanded the full force of the law. Did he lose his resolve, or was Aeschines seeking to make him look weak? This is one more instance in which the bare-knuckle style of Athenian orators, who retailed lies to boost themselves and tear down opponents, leaves the modern historian at a loss. One thing is clear: Demosthenes' growing prominence was making him enemies, and powerful ones at that.

By the late spring of 348, Olynthus's situation had become desperate. The two thousand mercenaries sent by Athens the previous year under Chares had achieved little; four thousand more, commanded by Charidemus, had joined them and had reclaimed some ground from Philip but had not relieved Olynthus. Athens at last acted with real urgency. The Assembly voted to send a third force: citizen troops in large numbers, two thousand infantry and three hundred cavalry, to be conveyed in seventeen ships, accompanied by horse transports. The Theoric Fund was not tapped — in this, Demosthenes had not succeeded — but the commitment to saving Olynthus was nonetheless impressive.

Once again, though, the yearly Etesian winds came to the aid of Philip. These northerlies kept the Athenian ships in port during crucial weeks in midsummer. Olynthus's resistance began to crumble. Two of its cavalry commanders went over to Philip's side and brought with them five hundred horsemen, sealing the city's doom. Before the third Athenian force could arrive, Olynthus had fallen.

Philip intended the fate of Olynthus to be a lesson to all who might choose to resist him. The population was not only enslaved but deported to Macedon to work the mines and perform other perilous tasks. The city itself was razed to the ground. Some years later Demosthenes would claim, no doubt hyperbolically, that no one could discern that the place had ever seen habitation.

Athens had done too little at first and then, after its measures failed, augmented them too slowly. The city had lost vital interests to Philip in both the Chalcidice and Euboea, and still had little hope of regaining Amphipolis. Since the Assembly's declaration of a war for that city, nine years earlier, few things had gone well for Athens. The Athenians' failures to meet the challenge of Philip, first in Thrace and then in the Chalcidice, had left them demoralized.

Small wonder then that the mood of Athens brightened when word arrived, even before the fall of Olynthus, that Philip wanted to work out a treaty of peace. That message prompted a flurry of diplomatic missions, amid which Demosthenes would find new ways to advance, as well as a new, and grimly determined, foe.

CHAPTER FOUR

None of Us Was Willing to Dine with Him

Aeschines of Sphettus had become politically prominent by 348, when he was appointed to lead a diplomatic mission to the Peloponnese. He was in his early forties at that time, perhaps a few years older than Demosthenes. He had sprung from undistinguished stock, the son of a schoolteacher father, Atrometus, and his wife, Glaucothea – or so he claimed. According to Demosthenes, though, Aeschines had been bred from the foulest mud. In a rhetorical sally against his rival, Demosthenes made the man's parents out to be the very dregs of society. He depicted Glaucothea first as a kind of witch, practicing strange religious rites with a band of occultists, and later, in one of his lowest blows, as a cheap whore.

These different accounts of Aeschines' origins highlight the problem for the biographer of writing about Greek rhetoricians of the classical age. In the no-holds-barred world of Athenian oratory, which lacked fact-checkers or gatekeepers, and in jury trials that lacked judges, slandering one's opponent with wild exaggerations or outright lies was the quickest route to success (a problem that persists in today's democracies). During two major showdowns in front of the demos, Demosthenes and Aeschines assailed one another with deadly rhetorical barbs, some no doubt freely invented. The speeches surviving from these duels are our best source for the two men's careers, yet those speeches are riddled with monstrous untruths. To pick out facts from the mass of competing claims is a challenging task.

Aeschines had been sent to the Peloponnese in 348 to organize Greek resistance to Philip. Athens was reaching out for allies in its Amphipolis war, but found, to its dismay, that many cities inclined more toward Philip than Athens. Some saw Philip as the defender of Delphi, whereas Athens had taken the Phocian side and dishonored Apollo; others were counting on benefits or bequests that Philip had promised. Aeschines returned from his mission empty-handed, and Athens pivoted from war to negotiation. Lacking the means to fight for Amphipolis, Athenians looked instead for a freeze in the conflict, a breathing space during which they might build up resources.

Having heard rumors that Philip too wanted a truce, a man named Philocrates started proposing an outreach to the Macedonian king. Assembly debate over this idea became more urgent after the fall of Olynthus. Philip captured Athenian troops there, and instead of selling them into slavery, held them as hostages. The Assembly soon thereafter adopted Philocrates' measure, appointing ten envoys to journey north and open a parley with Philip. Other Greek states wanted a seat at that parley and a role in whatever agreement emerged, but Demosthenes made sure that they were left out. Philip considered a Common Peace, contracted with all the Greek states, a nonstarter, so Demosthenes pragmatically scuttled the idea — a move that was later held against him.

The Assembly appointed both Aeschines and Demosthenes to

the board of ten envoys to Philip; they would be its two youngest members. In that moment these two rising speakers were on the same side. Both wanted assurances from Philip that Athens was safe and that Macedonian forces would stay out of central Greece, which meant staying north of the pass of Thermopylae. But their views of Philip, it soon emerged, diverged widely. Demosthenes had not abandoned his anti-Philip position; he saw the proposed treaty, now known as the Peace of Philocrates, as merely a pause in an ongoing conflict. Aeschines and his allies were more inclined to trust Philip and to see the Peace as a way that Athens might profit, trading compliance for grants of territory, perhaps for long-sought Amphipolis.

Appointment as envoy brought Demosthenes face-to-face, for the first time, with the man he had inveighed against for years. Anticipation must have been high for those in the room in Pella where the parley took place, especially for Demosthenes himself. We have only one report as to what transpired there, and it comes from a hostile witness, Aeschines.

In a later speech attacking Demosthenes, Aeschines claimed that the ten envoys had decided among themselves that on reaching Philip's capital city they would speak before Philip in order of age. That put the youngest, Demosthenes, last. Demosthenes had been boasting to his colleagues during their journey that he would "sew up Philip's mouth with unsoaked flax," that is, have an easy time silencing Philip (without needing to soak the flax to make it more limber), and would get Amphipolis back. Yet when his turn to speak arrived, Demosthenes came a cropper. "This creature," Aeschines sneered, using a word that denoted a wild animal, "spoke some prologue that was both obscure and lifeless with fright; he briefly recounted the chain of events from the start, then suddenly fell silent, became helpless, and finally abandoned the attempt to speak."[1]

Philip gently prodded Demosthenes to give it another try, reported Aeschines, but the orator crumpled again. After an embarrassed silence, Philip's herald gave the sign for the envoys to withdraw, and the interview ended.

Are we to trust this damning portrait of a cowardly lion, who talked tough behind Philip's back but then became paralyzed in his presence? Plutarch chose not to believe it, or at least, he omitted it from his Life of Demosthenes. But Demosthenes himself never refuted it in any of his extant orations or gave his own account of what happened in Pella that day. The point has been made that when Aeschines told this story in court, his audience included other envoys who had been witnesses to the parley, so he must have been telling the truth. But would such men have called out a lie when they heard one, or would they have held their tongues while a colleague launched his attacks?

Aeschines went on to describe the aftermath of the treaty conference, in ways that further belittled his fellow envoy. He claimed that Demosthenes sulked at first over his failure and the slight Philip later gave him at a state dinner. But on the return trip to Athens, Demosthenes suddenly brightened up, made a joke about his own discomfiture, and fawned on the other envoys, trying to wheedle them into giving a good report of his conduct. Aeschines thus exploited Demosthenes' position at the bottom of the age ladder (though he himself was second youngest) by making him seem unformed and insecure. He said that Demosthenes taught him the meaning of a Greek insult, *palimbolos,* "course-reverser," one who tacks with the shifting wind.

Though Aeschines cannot always be trusted, Demosthenes *did* reverse course during the rounds of negotiations with Philip. He started out as a firm proponent of the peace treaty and a supporter of Philocrates, its chief sponsor. As a newly installed member of the

Boule (Council), the executive board that set the Assembly's agenda, Demosthenes helped ensure that the treaty hammered out in Pella and brought back to Athens was voted on and passed without much revision. But even before the ink was dry on the pact—though in fact such treaties were not signed but sworn to by solemn oaths, then inscribed on stone stelas—he began to distance himself from it and blame his colleagues, especially Aeschines. The reasons behind this shift, which resulted in the complete breakdown of his relations with Aeschines, require a close inspection.

Looming over Athenian outreach to Philip was the question of the Third Sacred War, begun ten years earlier when the Phocians occupied Delphi. As we saw, Athens was allied with Phocis to counterbalance the power of Thebes, whereas Philip had lately entered the war on the Theban side against Phocis. By 346 the Phocians' hired army was faltering, and it appeared that Philip would have the last say in how the war ended. But no one knew his intentions. At stake in the outcome was control of the pass of Thermopylae, the southern end of which—where Athens had once stopped Philip and might need to do so again—was in Phocian hands.

At one point in early 346, the Phocian leaders offered to hand their Thermopylae forts over to Athens, their ally, and Athens dispatched its warships to take possession. But just then the Phocian leadership changed, and the offer was revoked. The general now in charge of the forts, a man named Phalaecus, opened communications with Philip instead, hoping to swap his strongholds for safe passage out of the region for himself and his troops. It is hard to discern how far this deal had progressed, or how much Demosthenes knew about it, at the time Athens was forging its bargain with Philip over the Peace of Philocrates. In the midst of those negotiations, it became clear that Philip had gotten control of the pass and could move south at will into central Greece.

Other conditions were shifting too as the peace process went forward. The treaty approved by Athens called for both sides to keep what lands they possessed at the time the oaths were sworn. But Philip was on campaign in Thrace, attacking Athenian allies, when the ten Athenian envoys returned to his palace to gain his consent to the ratified treaty. Demosthenes, Aeschines, Philocrates, and the seven others cooled their heels for weeks in Pella while Philip stayed on the march, improving a position that would soon become status quo. At some point during those weeks, if not before, Demosthenes made up his mind that the deal being struck was a bad one.

Politicians in Athens were just as conscious of optics as their modern-day counterparts, and Demosthenes was a consummate politician. He must have foreseen that Athenians would feel short-changed by the treaty and look for scapegoats, and he, as the youngest member of the embassy team, might well be their victim. So he shifted his ground and made himself an opponent of the treaty, while thrusting blame for its poor outcome onto others, especially his colleague Aeschines. Over the next fifteen years, the ways the two men handled themselves in regard to the Peace of Philocrates would be the subject of charges and countercharges, culminating in an all-out, bare-knuckle legal showdown.

According to Aeschines (but, again, his account is biased), the rest of the envoys already mistrusted Demosthenes when they again headed north. "None of us was willing to dine with him when we went on the second mission, or to lodge at the same inn, if it was possible not to do so," Aeschines later said.[2] When Philip finally joined the envoys in Pella and agreed to hear their speeches, Demosthenes, apparently now no longer intimidated, brashly insisted on speaking first. Then, according to Aeschines — again describing a palimbolos who shifts with the wind — Demosthenes used his speaking time to flatter Philip and tout the benefits he had done him in Athens, so cravenly as to raise a laugh from all present. Demosthenes surely told a different story, but we have no account from him of his speech on either this occasion or the previous one.

We do know that on this second visit, Demosthenes tried to gain the release of Athenian prisoners of war from Olynthus, still in Philip's hands after nearly two years. Seemingly without consulting his colleagues, he had brought a talent of silver for loans to captives who needed to make ransom payments; ultimately he converted the loans to gifts. Demosthenes had only enough for a few men however, and he urged Philip to free the rest. But Philip demurred, saying he would wait for the upcoming Panathenaia (an important Athenian state festival). Demosthenes had no doubt expected something like this, but his ploy had given him useful political leverage. He could now more plausibly argue to Athens that Philip could not be trusted; he was keeping Athenian citizens hostage, just as he was hanging on to Amphipolis.

The question of the prisoners impinged on the durability of the Peace, for under its terms, Athens had to send troops to serve under Philip in ending the Sacred War. Philip had insisted on this clause, and no sooner had he sworn to the treaty in his army camp near Thermopylae than he tried to put it into practice. Demosthenes saw yet another way to put Philip in the wrong; he could claim that the levy of troops was the monarch's attempt to gain *more* hostages. We are told that he tried to send a letter to the Assembly making this case, but his fellow ambassadors, aided by Philip, blocked the communiqué. The treaty's backers recognized that the pact would succeed only if Athens fulfilled this military obligation.

Demosthenes was playing a subtle game. A few weeks earlier, he had helped get the Peace of Philocrates passed and sent to Philip for ratification. But during those weeks the ground had shifted, and Philip had become more of a threat. Nothing prevented Philip now from joining with Thebes, his ally in the Sacred War, to create an anti-Athenian axis and dominate all of Hellas north of the Peloponnese. Athens was too weak to fight him, Demosthenes knew, but he could foresee that someday it would need to do so. The Peace, he resolved, must be only a pause, and also, to the extent that it gave away more than it gained, it must appear to be his colleagues' work, not his own.

When the ten envoys reached Athens, they made their report to the Boule as required. What they said is not known, but they must have made clear that things had gone badly, for they were not granted the honors or the state dinner usually conferred on returning ambassadors. According to Demosthenes, such a thing had never happened before in all of Athenian history. His own report to the Boule, perhaps, had made clear that no celebrations were needed since Athens had made a bad deal.

With the Peace of Philocrates now concluded and the Sacred War in its final stage, the Athenians again sent their envoys to Philip, to cement the new pact and offer their help in resolving the war. They had meant to send the same ten men as before, but Demosthenes refused to take part. He had had enough of talking to Philip and wanted to speak instead to the Assembly, presumably to undermine the new peace. Aeschines, though chosen to go with the others, declared himself too ill to travel and even produced a physician to certify this claim. Since he recovered quickly enough to take part in a fourth mission shortly thereafter, we might well suspect that his doctor's note was contrived.

What accounts for Aeschines' decision to stay home, just when Demosthenes had made the same choice? Demosthenes later claimed, perhaps plausibly, that Aeschines and his pro-treaty allies did not want to leave their chief opponent alone in the city, the better to work against them. Political lines were becoming clearer in Athens, with those on one side hoping to gain from entente with Philip, perhaps even get Amphipolis back, and those on the other resenting Philip for having (in their eyes) cheated them. Seldom before had Athens been so badly divided on a foreign policy issue. The split would be resolved only after nearly two decades of rhetorical battles, played out in both the Assembly and the courts.

The question the city first had to face was Philip's request for troops to help him in prosecuting the Sacred War. Philip had written letters to the Assembly from his camp near Thermopylae, making clear that he expected this provision to be fulfilled, but the Assembly declined. Perhaps Demosthenes influenced the decision by arguing that Philip really wanted more hostages. In any case, the demurral showed that the Peace, just a few weeks old, was already on uncertain footing.

The envoys from Athens were still en route north when they learned that the Phocians had surrendered – to Philip rather than to the Amphictyony. Their choice acknowledged that Philip, not the Greek cities that first declared war, was now to be the arbiter of the war's resolution. Philip had to walk a fine line in this role so as not to alienate either Athens or Thebes; both were now his allies, but hostile to one another and hopeful of different outcomes. Thebes would have liked to see all the male Phocians hurled from the top of the cliffs that loomed over Delphi, the punishment laid out for those who defiled the shrine. Athens, ever wary of Theban expansion, wanted Phocis preserved as a bulwark against Thebes.

The ten envoys returned to Athens as soon as they learned that the war was over but then were sent out again to take part in deliberations over its resolution. Aeschines returned to the team, while Demosthenes once more declined to serve. Aeschines later claimed that he played a key role in softening Philip and preventing the annihilation of Phocis, but he doubtless exaggerated his influence. Philip spared the lives of the Phocians but saddled them with heavy fines, to be used in restoring the wealth of Delphi; other measures ensured they could never again pose a threat to the shrine or their neighbors.

Philip was duly rewarded for his rescue of Delphi with coveted honors, including *promanteia*, the right to go first when consulting the oracle, and headship of the Pythian athletic games then in the offing. More important, two of the twelve seats on the Amphictyonic board, those formerly held by Phocis, were awarded to Philip. With the other votes that he indirectly controlled, Philip could henceforth sway the decisions by which the shrine was managed and sacred wars were declared. He could use the board as a weapon against his Greek foes — including Athens, if he so chose, for Athens had (before a last-minute shift) supported the Phocians in their illegal war effort. Indeed the Athenians briefly manned their defenses, as though expecting attack, when they heard of Phocis's surrender. Their new accord with Philip was *that* fragile and trust in his intentions *that* low.

Soon after the well-traveled envoys returned to Athens from their fourth mission, Demosthenes, now firmly convinced that the Peace was unpopular, filed suit against Aeschines on a charge of *parapresbeia* — usually translated "false embassy." His argument was that Aeschines had taken bribes from Philip to act against Athenian interests and bring about a bad treaty. Demosthenes was seeking to make Aeschines take the fall for a deal that might otherwise be blamed on *him*.

Demosthenes brought in as his co-accuser an ally named Timarchus. Aeschines fought back by attacking Timarchus in a suit of his own, from which his speech "Against Timarchus" survives.

Aeschines' own trial on the "false embassy" charge did not take place until several years later, when he and Demosthenes fought one another directly. First they did battle by proxy. Demosthenes wrote the speech Timarchus used to defend himself and also, most likely, appeared at the trial as a character witness. Aeschines, for his part, tried to spatter so much mud on Timarchus that some of it would, inevitably, befoul Demosthenes too.

In ancient Greek politics, as in those of modern societies, nothing besmirched an opponent quite so well as scandalous sex. The Greeks were largely accepting of male-male erotic relationships, but even so there were sexual roles that they saw as unseemly for men, especially men who aspired to leadership. The role of *pornos*, "whore," in which a man sold his body to other men, was one of these, especially if combined with passivity, promiscuity, and the effeminacy the Greeks attributed to the bottom, or penetrated, partner. In prosecuting Timarchus, Aeschines dragged all these sexual bugbears into public view. He relied on an Athenian law that forbade men who sold their bodies, or behaved in various other dissolute ways, from speaking in the Assembly or holding office. Timarchus, he claimed, had violated this law by exercising his citizen rights.

Aeschines began his review of Timarchus's sexual history by apologizing for the things he would have to say. "You would not justly blame *me*, if I should speak candidly . . . but rather *him*, if he happens to have lived so foully as to make it impossible for one describing his deeds to speak as he wishes," Aeschines told the jurors. Even after giving himself this license, Aeschines went on to allude to acts too lurid to mention. In his summation he referred to "womanish sins" and claimed that Timarchus had "inflicted outrages upon himself, in violation of nature," leaving specifics to the jury's imagination.[3]

According to Aeschines' account, Timarchus had sold himself to a series of disreputable lovers, including — vilest of all — a city-owned slave by the name of Pittalacus. In between these sordid affairs, Timarchus had wasted his income, as well as his patrimony, on gambling, drinking, and other forms of loose living. The picture Aeschines painted was seamy enough to get Timarchus convicted and stripped of his citizen rights, an outcome that removed him from politics as well as from the "false embassy" prosecutorial team. But what interests us are the collateral salvos launched at Demosthenes in the course of the speech. Aeschines tried to tar his chief rival with the same brush he used on Timarchus, the most damning one he could find, as well as the one least subject to verification.

The effort to blend two deviant males together began with the topic of nicknames. Aeschines first claimed that Timarchus was so widely known for male prostitution that "pornos" had become his sobriquet. "The moment his name is spoken, you all ask the question, 'Which Timarchus? The whore?'" he told the jury, as though they regarded "pornos" as the man's last name. Then he moved on to Batalus, Demosthenes' nickname. Ignoring the standard meaning, "Stutterer," Aeschines invoked the alternative, "anus," by saying that those who call Demosthenes Batalus were referring to his *kinaidia*, "lascivious sexuality" with a "bottom" orientation. Elsewhere in the speech Aeschines labeled Demosthenes a *kinaidos*, a man who (perversely in Greek eyes) craved being penetrated, and, in another speech, an androgyne.[4]

The vitriol behind these smears arose out of Aeschines' sense of betrayal. That much is clear from a sentence in which Aeschines cast his rival as an effeminate, a wearer of lush, pretty garments more typical of women than men. Addressing Demosthenes directly, he mocked "those soft little tunics you wear when you compose your speeches against your friends."[5] Aeschines had thought himself one of those "friends" (a word that also connotes political alliance) right up until the "false embassy" suit. Indeed, he made the point in a later speech that Demosthenes had sandbagged him, praising him when they both returned from their first diplomatic mission only to denounce him after the fourth.

Somehow, between the first and last embassies, a span of perhaps four months, Demosthenes had turned on his next-youngest colleague, making him out to be a traitor and taker of bribes. To Aeschines this must have felt like a stab in the back. The sting fueled his anger and, later, his quest for revenge.

As the turbulent summer of 346 turned to autumn, envoys from Philip arrived in Athens, accompanied by others from Thessaly, Philip's staunch ally. They were seeking approval of Philip's take-over of the two Phocian seats on the Amphictyonic board. In effect, Philip wanted the blessing of Athens for what was already decided. The debate over this request brought Demosthenes again to the bema, where he delivered the speech now known as "On the Peace."

To judge by this speech, Athenians at that moment felt dangerously isolated. Their support of Phocis in the Sacred War had put them at odds with both Thebes and Thessaly, and their long-standing embrace of Sparta had alienated the many Peloponnesians who hated the Spartans. Any small provocation might ignite a war in which most of Greece, plus Philip, could join in attacking Athens. The idea of fighting to gain Amphipolis was by now a distant mirage; Athens might need to fight for its very survival.

Demosthenes took the occasion to reflect on the recent treaty negotiations, again accusing his fellow envoys — not named in this instance — of pocketing Philip's bribes. He claimed that he alone had told the truth about the Peace while others encouraged false hopes. His foresight, he said modestly, came not from intelligence but first from good luck, a more valuable asset than wits, and second from the fact that he could not be bought. "No one could show any gains connected to things I've said or policies I've supported," he claimed, a point that would later be hotly disputed.[6] With Aeschines clearly in mind, he compared political decision making to a pair of scales; add silver to one of its pans, and the pan tips away from sound judgment and reason.

Turning to the treaty itself, Demosthenes again acknowledged its flaws but did not advise the Athenians to break it. "Whatever sort of peace it is, better for our affairs that it had never been made than, once it's been made, we now violate it," he said in a deliberately opaque sentence.[7] His position was a complex one, requiring twists of logic: he needed to argue both that the Peace should never have been passed and that Athenians, in their weak strategic position, would be fools to abrogate it.

In closing the speech, Demosthenes, in an uncharacteristic concession, urged the Assembly to give Philip what he wanted rather than start a fight. Already Athens had had to accept the loss of Amphipolis, the destruction of Olynthus, the defeat of its ally Phocis, and the surrender of the Thermopylae pass; anointing Philip as an Amphictyon was a small setback by comparison. For the moment, the city had to swallow its pride and go along with Philip's elevation.

Demosthenes was being pragmatic, but he also held on to hopes that Athens would one day fight for the freedom of Greece. It would not be long before those hopes were fulfilled.

CHAPTER FIVE

You Haven't Been Defeated, for You Haven't so Much as Stirred

In Athens and other assembly-run cities, decisions on foreign policy were made much the way jury verdicts are today. Citizens listened to envoys from elsewhere and to their own rhetoricians, each side telling them how they should view a particular policy choice, where their best interests lay, and what mistakes they were making in reading others' intentions. Their votes were partly based on whom they most liked or trusted (or least *mistrusted*). Speakers not only made their own cases but also assailed their opponents, usually, and often with reason, alleging bribery or ulterior motives. Integrity, or at least its appearance, was a vital asset for those who mounted the bema.

Since alliances between states were constantly shifting in Demosthenes' day, assemblies had lots of practice listening to such speeches and sorting out the plausible from the mendacious. Those in powerful cities learned to anticipate the plans of rivals (if they were unable to glean them from informants and spies). The task of discerning Philip's intentions, however, posed a new challenge to Greek decision makers. They found that a monarch with only a small inner circle who moved his forces about without need of debate was far more opaque than the citizenries they normally dealt with. In conclaves across the Greek world, arguments raged over what Philip intended, where he might turn, and which cities he would befriend or which oppose.

What Philip had in mind for Athens, and central Greece generally, was especially hard to analyze (and still is). After ending the Sacred War he had withdrawn from the region, and many supposed that he meant to stay out, except for indirect meddling. Some Athenians, Aeschines among them, hoped that by playing along with Philip they might make huge gains, even get back Amphipolis in some kind of swap, and at the same time ensure the reduction of their regional rival, Thebes. An even more optimistic faction, led by Isocrates, saw in Philip a savior who could unite the fractious Greeks under a single banner. In a speech published just after the Peace of Philocrates was concluded, Isocrates hailed Philip as a descendant of Heracles, thereby affirming his Greek identity, and urged him to lead a crusade against the Great King of Persia. Behind him, Isocrates wrote, the Greeks could band together against a barbarian foe.

Demosthenes stood at the opposite pole from these hopeful or even utopian assessments. In all Philip's moves, especially those at the end of the Sacred War, he saw growing danger to Athens and all of Greece. In his "Third Olynthiac," Demosthenes had already called Philip a barbaros, a non-Greek, and he soon revived that term of opprobrium. Such an outsider could lead the Greeks, he felt, only by becoming their overlord. It was Philip, in Demosthenes' eyes, not the Persian Great King, against whom the city-states had to unite when war arrived, as he believed it must do.

Was Demosthenes right to mistrust Philip, or had he, as one scholar puts it, "raised paranoia to an art form"?[1] Should he be seen as a brave defender of freedom, or as a fearmonger who misled his nation, who stoked bias and hatred to boost his own career? Answers to these questions have varied widely in modern times, depending largely on changing views of Philip. When seen as a statesman and nation-builder, the founding father of a united Greece, Philip looks like a positive force and Demosthenes a fool for resisting him. But when seen as a ruthless conqueror, Philip resembles, and has been compared to, a modern fascist dictator, and the cause of Demosthenes seems correspondingly noble. Recent decades have seen opinion shift in Philip's favor, a trend that puzzled the classicist Philip Harding. "In so many ways Demosthenes is a man for our times — the very model of a modern democratic politician," he wrote in 2000; "Could it be that his unpopularity reflects our own feelings about the politicians of our day?"[2]

In the war that he sensed was coming, Demosthenes knew that the Thebans, with their formidable infantry, would play a critical role. The Thebans were currently Philippizing but not with conviction; at one point near the end of the Sacred War, when Philip had excluded them from his counsels, they had mobilized troops to resist an attack, just as Athens had done at almost the same moment. The two leading cities of Greece, one a land power, the other strong at sea, had much to gain from collaboration, but decades of enmity split them apart. Demosthenes was one of few in Athens committed to decent relations with Thebes; Aeschines even accused him of being a Theban *proxenos*, an agent paid to defend Theban interests in Athens. If Demosthenes really had such a role, he kept it quiet, knowing how much his countrymen disliked the Thebans. The time would come when he would ask them to reverse their opinion.

The states of the Peloponnese were a better prospect as allies for Athens, even though they had shown little interest in opposing

Philip. Aeschines had sounded them out in his first diplomatic assignment in 348, before the peace effort began. He had had no success on that outing, but five years later Demosthenes, chosen by the Assembly to serve as its spokesman, journeyed southward to try his own luck. His speeches from that mission do not survive, but he quoted from them in a speech he delivered at Athens soon after returning.

When he had addressed the citizens of Messene, in the west of the Peloponnese, Demosthenes (by his own report) had evoked the fate of Olynthus, destroyed by Philip some seven or eight years earlier. The Olynthians, he said, had trusted Philip, just as the Messenians were doing at that moment. But Olynthus had been reduced to rubble by the treacherous Philip. Demosthenes then cast the struggle with Philip in ideological terms. "These too-close links to tyrants are dangerous for constitutional states," he declared; the Olynthians had been morally undermined by their dealings with Philip.[3] For the first time (as far as we know) in his speaking career, Demosthenes labeled Philip a *turannos*, "tyrant" or "despot," though most Greeks would have called him *basileus*, "king."

Demosthenes recurred to the contrast between forms of government in his peroration (as he later reported). "What are you looking for – Freedom?" he asked the Messenians, whose population was largely made up of freed Spartan serfs. "Then don't you see that Philip's very titles are opposed to this goal? For every king and tyrant" – he lumped the two terms for sole rulers together – "is an enemy to freedom and a foe to the rule of law. Beware lest, in seeking to avoid a war, you find a slave master."[4] The Messenians, Demosthenes later claimed, had roared out their approval, but when the time came for policy votes, they elected to stick by Philip. Philip had promised them aid and protection from Sparta, and they believed him.

The question of whether promises would be kept was much on the minds of Athenians too in the late 340s. The envoys who supported the Peace of Philocrates had told the Assembly that Philip had promised great things, but as two and then three years passed, few benefactions arrived. Anger against the treaty and Philip was growing, stoked of course by Demosthenes and his allies – who now included a newly prominent orator, Hyperides. Philip's efforts to mollify Athens by having the treaty altered brought a new round of diplomatic exchanges and Assembly debates, all of which came to nothing. Philip refused to give as much as Athenian hard-liners demanded, and the demos chose not to accept what it saw as half measures.

As resentment of Philip grew, the anti-Macedon faction at Athens lashed out once more, as it had in 346, against those who had fostered the Peace. This time it was not Demosthenes leading the charge but Hyperides, an even fiercer firebrand, a man well known in Athens for his wealth and flamboyant pleasure seeking. Though his hedonist ways set him strongly apart from Demosthenes the water drinker, the two orators were to be partners and friends over the next two decades, until the currents of change bore them in opposing directions.

Hyperides chose as his target Philocrates, who first proposed the treaty that today bears his name. Employing the move known as *eisangelia,* by which an indictment could be announced before the Assembly, Hyperides stood at the bema and charged Philocrates with taking Philip's bribes – the same indictment Demosthenes had brought against Aeschines, in a case still awaiting trial. By his own account Demosthenes rose at that moment, no doubt by prearrangement, and said that Hyperides' charge was lacking in one respect: it did not include *other* envoys who had also been on the take. "Let any man who wishes stand up, come forward, and declare before you all that he took no part in Philocrates' actions and does not approve them," Demosthenes told the Assembly, no doubt looking straight at Aeschines. "I will release from prosecution anyone who does this."[5] None of Philocrates' factional allies chose to desert.

This public display of aggression was enough to frighten Philocrates. He fled the city and went into exile before his case came to trial. Hyperides prosecuted him in absentia and obtained an easy conviction and sentence of death. Another huge blow had been struck against the Peace: repudiation of its principal author.

Encouraged by this victory for his faction, and perhaps not wanting to be outshone by an eloquent rival, Demosthenes strode once more into political combat. He revived his long-dormant indictment of Aeschines for his "false embassy" at the court of Philip. Unlike Philocrates, Aeschines chose to stay in Athens and stand his ground with a speech of self-defense. A battle of star orators took shape, with the fate of the Peace, and of the city's relations with Philip, enmeshed in the outcome.

The trial took place before a jury of hundreds, perhaps a thousand, with many more spectators watching from beyond a barrier fence. Aeschines noted in his defense speech (which survives) that a majority of the demos, a body that numbered upward of thirty thousand, was in attendance that day. Perhaps this was an exaggeration, but it *was* a climactic case, a high-profile fight between two top Athenian leaders. It was also a grudge match, since Aeschines had bitterly struck at Demosthenes in "Against Timarchus" three years earlier. In his prosecutorial speech, now known as "On the False Embassy," Demosthenes showed that he was determined to give as good as he'd gotten. If we trust Aeschines, he went so far in his vitriol as to draw shouts of outrage from the mob of onlookers present.

As Aeschines had done in the Timarchus trial, Demosthenes looked back in "On the False Embassy" to events at Pella, the Macedonian capital, when the envoys had first arrived to talk to Philip — events to which, conveniently, very few Athenians had been witness. In the earlier trial, Aeschines had told the highly damaging story about how Demosthenes had crumpled in Philip's presence and could not produce any words. Demosthenes took his revenge in "On the False Embassy" with a lurid account of Aeschines' behavior at a party in Macedon.

Aeschines and some friends, Demosthenes claimed, were drinking at a banquet in Pella thrown by an Athenian living in exile. The host brought into the room a young Greek woman who had been captured in the fall of Olynthus and brought to Macedon, no doubt as a concubine. The drunken feasters demanded that the woman sing them a song, but she refused, explaining that she had no musical talent. Aeschines and his friend demanded a whip to be fetched, then stood by as the woman was stripped and flogged mercilessly. The sordid scene, Demosthenes claimed, had at the time become a scandal, talked of clear across Greece.[6]

Whether Demosthenes dredged up the story or invented it, he had found a highly effective line of attack. The behavior he described, combining drunkenness, arrogance, and cruelty, was the hallmark of the tyrannical soul, one that lacked the virtue of *sophrosune*, "self-restraint." A man with such a soul would ally himself with tyrants or even try to become a tyrant himself. The fact that the victim came from Olynthus, the city that more than any other evoked Philip's ruthlessness, gave the story greater point and meaning. By implication it tied Aeschines and Philip together as twin assailants of the Olynthians.

In his defense speech, also referred to as "On the False Embassy," Aeschines twice denounced Demosthenes for the tale of the

Olynthian woman, citing it as an example of mendacity. He even produced a deposition from an Olynthian man who claimed that Demosthenes paid him a thousand drachmas to back up the story.[7] But Aeschines was himself well-versed in character assassination, as we have seen. In his own "On the False Embassy," he shot further darts at Demosthenes' sexual habits and several times maintained – with no attempt at proof – that his opponent's mother was no Athenian but a Scythian nomad from the Eurasian steppes. If that had been true, Demosthenes would have been a noncitizen, ineligible to bring any legal action – but no one, not even Aeschines, made a case for his exclusion.

The larger issue on which the two men divided was of course the Peace of Philocrates, now reviled by many at Athens after Philip's gains under its aegis. Demosthenes cast Aeschines as a firm supporter of the Peace and therefore of Philip, suggesting that Philip had even employed Aeschines to write a letter to Athens on his behalf. Aeschines, in his rebuttal, made little attempt to defend the Peace but argued that Demosthenes had backed the treaty at first and helped get it passed before reversing positions. Both men went back over all the old ground of their embassies to Philip, their Assembly speeches, and their political actions three years earlier. Athenians had by this time heard so many accounts of this sequence that few, no doubt, could be sure of who had said what at various times or who was more brazenly stretching the truth at the trial.

When the time arrived for the jury to cast their ballots, Aeschines was acquitted by thirty votes. He had convinced a bare majority that he had not taken bribes from Philip or acted improperly in his diplomatic role. All the same, the nearly even vote showed that Demosthenes had built an effective case and had scored many hits. His efforts to cast the peace treaty as the product of perfidy was far from concluded; the same was true of his duel with Aeschines.

In the late 340s Philip's son Alexander was in his early teens. To get him properly educated, Philip called in an old friend, a Greek who had grown up at Pella as the son of the royal physician. Aristotle was at this time a student in Plato's Academy and therefore, though not an Athenian citizen, a member of the intellectual elite who called Athens home. By hiring this man to tutor his heir apparent, Philip signaled to all the Greeks his reverence for "the school of Hellas" — the phrase Pericles had once used in extolling the culture of Athens.

But valuing Athenian culture did not necessarily mean respecting Athenian interests. While Alexander and his friends were sequestered with Aristotle, Philip was on the move in Thrace at the head of an army. His campaign there in 342 and 341 convinced many in Athens that his intentions were hostile; it seemed designed to create a chokehold on the waterways through which Black Sea grain was shipped to Greece. Elderly Athenians still remembered how they had starved in 404 when the Spartans had interdicted the grain trade and forced them to sign a humiliating surrender. It was easy for them, and for their progeny, to imagine that Philip was making a similar play.

Other developments just off Attica's coast were also rattling Athenian nerves at this time. The island of Euboea had in the past been firmly attached to Athens, but during the mid-340s Philippizing regimes took power in some of its cities. No one could say for certain how big a role Philip played in these shifts; his agents were everywhere in the Greek world, distributing bribes and supporting his puppets, so there was cause for suspicion. But in 342 Philip acted more openly, sending troops to support his Euboean allies and to ensure that their pro-Athenian rivals stayed far from power. Though this did not technically violate the Peace — no governments were forcibly overturned – the infringement Athenians felt was very real.

Amid the growing anger in Athens at Philip, with Philocrates exiled and Aeschines on the back foot, Demosthenes stepped up once again to the forefront. The case he had long been making, that Philip could not be trusted and that the Peace of Philocrates was a sham, increasingly seemed like the right way to look at events. In Assembly speeches he gave in 341, Demosthenes hit those themes hard and often, trying to ready his city for what he thought was now inescapable: war. Two of these speeches have been preserved, probably in versions Demosthenes edited after he gave them and then published for wide circulation. Two other surviving anti-Philip speeches, dating to 340, are probably, but less certainly, the work of Demosthenes.

The speech now called "On the Chersonese" addressed Athenians' fears over the long Thracian peninsula, the Chersonese (now called Gallipoli), that Athens used as a base for protecting its Black Sea trade. Settlers had been sent there from Athens, and an Athenian soldier of fortune, Diopeithes, had undertaken to guard them, relying on hired mercenaries. To pay his men's wages Diopeithes plundered places in Thrace that belonged to Macedon, prompting Philip to send an angry letter to Athens. "On the Chersonese" was Demosthenes' response. In it he argued that Philip had already broken the Peace and should be dealt with accordingly. Rather than appease him by reining in Diopeithes, the city should be raising money through taxes, preparing a new force to send to Thrace, and brutally suppressing the voices in Athens of those "who have sold themselves to Philip" (implying, no doubt, Aeschines).[8]

"What are we waiting for?" Demosthenes asked the Assembly. "Or when, Athenians, will we be willing to do what is needed? 'When we are forced to, by Zeus,'" he imagined his hearers replying. "But if we speak of the force used on free men, it's not only already here, it arrived a long time ago. As to the force used on slaves, we must surely pray that *that* never happens. . . . It's not even fit to be spoken of!"[9]

The horrors of enslavement were terrifying enough, but Demosthenes went on to argue that Athens would suffer a worse fate under Philip – annihilation. "The danger is not the same for you as it is for others," he claimed. "Philip does not want to make you his subjects, but to utterly destroy you. He knows well that you won't be willing to be slaves, nor, if you *are* willing, will you know how – for you are accustomed to rule. You will be able to give him more trouble than all the rest of humankind."[10] It is hard for us to determine whether Demosthenes believed these predictions or found them a useful scare tactic. In the end (as we'll see) Philip *did* make an exception for Athens, by treating it *better* than other opponents.

Philip wrote again to the Assembly, perhaps having learned of Demosthenes' words from informants. In his new letter Philip claimed that he was *not* at war with Athens, or with any other Greek state that accepted Macedonian power. "My stance is peace toward all those willing to heed me," he wrote, in a sentence Demosthenes quoted.[11] He may indeed have been hoping to leave central Greece undisturbed, for his larger objective, probably taking shape by that time, lay not to the south but to the east: Asia Minor, the rich western provinces of the vast Persian Empire. To get there, he needed a quiescent Greece at his rear, and also passage across the Hellespont, a waterway controlled by Athenian ships.

In his "Third Philippic," the most vehement of his surviving policy speeches, Demosthenes summoned all his rhetorical powers to reject Philip's outreach. He painted a dire picture of how Athens had failed through inaction. "I fear that it's true, though an ill-omened thing to say: even if all those mounting the bema had wished to speak, and you to vote, in such a way as to have your affairs turn out as badly as possible, I don't think those affairs could have been arranged any worse than they are right now," he inveighed in his opening sentence. Yet in this extreme of failure lay hope for the city, for the measures that might yet save it were still untried: "You haven't been defeated, for you haven't so much as stirred."[12]

Demosthenes had not used racial attacks against Philip since the "Third Olynthiac" eight years previously, but he brought them back with a vengeance in his "Third Philippic." Perhaps he was partly rebutting a rival opinion maker, Isocrates, who had recently published his fawning open letter to Philip. Isocrates claimed to be seeking a champion to lead the Greek fight against "the barbarians" — the Persians. Demosthenes, however, insisted, as he had earlier, that Philip himself was a barbaros, an intruder into Hellas. "Not only is he not a Greek, and in no way related to the Greeks, he's not even a barbaros from a place that one speaks of with pride; he's a vile Macedonian, hailing from where in the past one couldn't even purchase a decent slave!"[13]

In a memorable simile, Demosthenes likened Philip to a distant hailstorm making its way across the land, spreading destruction; all see the danger approaching but no one takes action, each hoping the storm will turn in a different direction.[14] (In the "Fourth Philippic," if that speech is his work, he compared the Greeks to stupefied sleepers who had drunk mandrake juice, a narcotic.) He urged Athens to send diplomats to all parts of Greece, and even to the Great King of Persia, to make common cause against Philip. But first, he said, the city had to set an example by raising funds and building ships, and by sending support to Diopeithes in the Chersonese.

The "Third Philippic" is light on the ideological themes Demosthenes highlighted elsewhere. Its case is built not on the moral strength of democracy or the need to fight tyrants but on the more basic issue of self-preservation. It also makes an appeal to Athenian historical greatness, which, in its author's view, conferred on Athens a special leadership role. "If you think that the Chalcidians or Megarians will save Greece," Demosthenes concluded, naming two less notable Greek populations, "and that you'll manage to shirk the task, you're mistaken. . . . It's *you* who must do this. Your ancestors won this prize by facing many great dangers, and bequeathed it to you."[15]

The words of the "Third Philippic" found their mark; the Assembly voted to send envoys to the other Greek states and to the Great King in Persia, Artaxerxes III, in hopes of building an anti-Philip coalition. The demos thus moved a giant step closer to launching a full-scale war. Thanks to the specters and fears Demosthenes had evoked, and the patriotism he summoned, Athenians would not stand by and pray that the hailstorm would turn nor would they drug themselves into a slumber. Before the storm hit, they would act.

CHAPTER SIX

I Alone Did Not Desert My Place

Democracies, as we know, must sometimes resort to anti-democratic measures in order to survive. Athens had acknowledged this paradox from the start of its history as a democracy. It incorporated into its constitution the procedure called ostracism, "potsherding," whereby the demos could vote to banish a single Athenian for a span of ten years. Votes were cast by means of a potsherd, or *ostrakon*, on which the name of the target could be scratched. By Demosthenes' time the procedure had fallen out of use, but its raison d'être – the polity's need under stress to act against internal threats without judicial proceedings – had not disappeared.

New measures arose over time by which the Athenians kept their constitution safe, even if it required the shedding of blood. In 410, a law passed by one Demophantus instituted an oath, to be sworn by all male citizens, that they would kill anyone who tried to overturn the democracy and that any such murders would not be considered a crime. As in the case of ostracism, the city was willing to trample on an individual's rights in order to safeguard those of the demos.

Then in the late 340s, Demosthenes moved a decree that gave the state greater powers of suppression. His motion allowed the judicial board known as the Areopagus to act on its sole authority, without consulting the Assembly, against those it suspected of wrongdoing. The Areopagus was a far more august body than any trial jury; its members, former officials in Athens, served life terms, as on the modern U.S. Supreme Court. Its brief to that point had included prosecutions for murder, but under the new decree it could try anyone for any crime and impose punishment on those it found guilty. The high court became a tribunal.

Demosthenes himself made use of the supercharged Areopagus to get several people banished or executed. The best-known case is that of Antiphon (not the orator of that name). This man, according to his accusers, had incurred a penalty in Athens and lost his citizen rights, then fled to the court of Philip; from there, it was claimed, he had slipped back into Piraeus with the intention of setting fire to the Athenian dockyards. Demosthenes, acting on his suspicions, had Antiphon hunted down. This manhunt went beyond the law, according to Aeschines, since Antiphon's quarters were entered without a warrant, though Demosthenes mocked that objection and boasted instead of his swiftness in acting.[1] The Assembly, in an initial proceeding, found no reason to charge Antiphon, but Demosthenes saw to it that the newly empowered Areopagus took the case. In the smaller body, where Demosthenes held greater sway, Antiphon was tortured to gain a confession, then sentenced to execution.

Other, less prominent figures went to their deaths or into exile by way of the new procedures. A certain Charinus was banished after making an Assembly motion that increased Athenian levies on the small Thracian town of Aenus. The town went over to Philip's side to avoid the heavier payment, and Charinus was therefore judged a traitor. Polyxenus, a descendant of the heroic tyrant slayer Harmodius, was thrown into prison for some unspecified crime. A priestess from Lemnos, Theoris, was executed along with her family when Demosthenes insisted on the death penalty. She had conducted suspicious mystical rites and also, obscurely, had "taught the slaves to deceive," according to Plutarch's account.[2]

These moves were later decried as abuses, after Demosthenes himself had been charged by the very body he had given such latitude. But Plutarch puts them in a more positive light. In his effort to see the best in Demosthenes, he characterizes the prosecution of Antiphon, in defiance of the Assembly, as part of an "aristocratic" style — in this context a positive attribute. "He opposed himself to the desires of the masses," Plutarch explains, echoing praise that Thucydides had long before bestowed on Pericles.[3] In this warped reckoning, the use of a small group of allies to gain convictions, in a circumvention of larger judicial bodies, is seen not as a misuse of power but high statesmanship.

Plutarch may have found Periclean echoes in this sidestepping of the Assembly and courts, but he also saw a huge gap between Demosthenes and his illustrious forerunner. Pericles had steered the Assembly while occupying the office of *strategos*, an elected military command; he, and the other great leaders of former days, had proved themselves on the battlefield as well as in verbal debates. But in the time after Pericles, the roles of rhetor and strategos had begun to diverge. Demosthenes belonged to a new political breed that amassed its power from words without deeds. Plutarch pauses at one point to voice his regret over this. "If only martial courage and integrity in his actions had been added to the ambition of his proposals and the nobility of his words, he would have been worthy of top rank, along with . . . Pericles."[4]

Paradoxically, this unmilitary man would, over the next few

years, lead the faction at Athens that pushed hard for war. By contrast, his opposite number, Phocion — who served as strategos dozens of times but who spoke before the Assembly in a brusque, unpolished manner — resented the rush toward war and argued for peaceful solutions. With his long field experience, Phocion was aware of what Athens needed, but lacked, for a fight against Philip. "It's not the *stadion* of war, but the *dolichon*, that concerns me," he said on one occasion, comparing a short footrace with a run nearly three miles long.[5]

However lopsided his talents, Demosthenes in the late 340s was at the apex of his influence. Owing to his motions in the Assembly, Athens sent forces to Euboea and reversed a coup engineered there by a tyrant aligned with Philip. This was the first direct challenge to Philip's power that Athens had mounted since the Peace of Philocrates had been signed, and it was soon followed by other moves to firm up Euboean alliances. Meanwhile, Demosthenes went in person as an envoy to the Peloponnese and to Byzantium, the city controlling the crucial Black Sea grain route. We have no record of what he said in those places, but he won new pacts of collaboration. He took a lead role in assembling a small but meaningful league against Philip.

At the Dionysia festival in Athens in March 340 a crier came forward before the throngs gathered to watch the tragic plays and presented Demosthenes with an honorific gold crown (his second). Such crowns were a standard way in which Athens officially thanked its benefactors and also signaled its policy choices. The highly public award made clear, not only to Athenians but to dignitaries from many places attending the festival, that Athenians endorsed Demosthenes' view of the world. Though they still adhered to Philocrates' treaty, they were inclined now to think that Philip was making war in the guise of peace.

Philip, it seems, thought the same about the Athenians. At least that was what he expressed in a letter to Athens, probably sent in the summer of 340. He had been writing such letters for years, complaining to Athens about perceived provocations, but only one missive has survived (assuming the one we have is authentic; doubts have been raised). In this public letter, we can see how badly trust had eroded between the two nominal allies and how close they were to a breach.

"Don't be surprised at the length of my letter; I have many charges to make," Philip wrote at the outset. He then listed a dozen or more arenas in which the Athenians disregarded his rights, treated him poorly, or ignored his efforts to find fair solutions. His final item returned to the very first point of dispute between him and Athens: Amphipolis. Athenian orators had not ceased to agitate for the return of this city; they assailed the Peace of Philocrates on the grounds that it implicitly gave Amphipolis away. Philip taunted the Assembly by claiming that he could bribe such men into taking *his* side in future. "It would be easy for me, by casting a little something their way, to stop their abuse and make them sing hymns of praise to us," he boasted, in a high-handed tone that Demosthenes must have found galling.[6]

Philip concluded the letter with a thinly veiled threat. "Since you began hostilities, and, through my forbearance, are continuing to attack my interests, and are doing me as much wrong as you are able, I shall defend myself with the aid of justice, and, making the gods my witnesses, I shall take in hand my disagreements with you."[7] His final words can be translated various ways; Philip no doubt meant them to be opaque. He did not want to be first to declare the Peace dead, though by his tone he showed that he believed it to be so.

The most disingenuous charge Philip made in the letter was that he had been forced, by attacks from Athenian settlers in the Chersonese, to send his army toward the Hellespont to protect his ships. In fact he was sending both troops and ships to assault Perinthus and Byzantium, two cities crucial to control of the straits. He complained as well of Athenian outreach toward the Great King, but that outreach had been prompted chiefly by his own eastward incursions. So Philip was making himself seem the victim where he was most the aggressor. His letter was sent while his army was still on the march and his military objective was still unclear; but when his army laid siege to Perinthus, no one in Athens could doubt any longer.

The attack on Perinthus raised alarms in the Persian Empire as well, for control of the straits would allow Philip's army to cross into Asia. No one as yet was sure whether Philip intended to make that crossing, as Isocrates urged him to do. But Artaxerxes decided to take preemptive action. He ordered his westernmost satraps to send aid across the Propontis (Sea of Azov) to bolster Perinthian resistance. The Byzantines, too, recognizing that their own fate was closely tied to that of their neighbors, dispatched squads of soldiers. The siege of Perinthus, unlike Philip's earlier sieges, became an entrenched stalemate that went on for months.

Engineers hired by Philip had by this time greatly improved his siege machines and artillery weapons. His torsion catapults and crossbows, driven by twisted bundles of hair, rained rocks and metal bolts on Perinthus, while an enormous wheeled tower, over a hundred feet high, was rolled up to the walls, allowing his men to shoot down into the town. With his army of thirty thousand working in relays, Philip kept up pressure on the Perinthians day and night, exhausting their stamina. Observers were awed at the first full-scale deployment of Philip's new siege train. A section of the Perinthian wall was destroyed, but the town's inhabitants quickly blocked off lanes and used frontline houses to raise a new barricade. Reinforcements kept arriving from Byzantium to take the place of fallen Perinthians, forcing Philip to divide his forces and put Byzantium under siege as well – a second assault on vital Athenian interests. Meanwhile the aid sent by Persia began to flow by sea to Perinthus, convincing Philip that capturing it was now impossible. Byzantium too, with its strong defenses, looked to be holding out; Philip was stymied on two fronts, an embarrassment in the eyes of the watching Greeks. But then he spotted a chance to restore his reputation with one swift stroke.

This was the time of the harvest in what is now Ukraine, and merchant fleets were making their way through the straits, bringing cargoes of grain to Athens and other cities. Athenian warships were present to escort them; but when their commander was briefly off the scene, Philip contrived to seize the entire fleet of more than two hundred vessels. In a punitive gesture, he held on to the ships bound for Athens and let the others proceed. Athenians would be forced to face a year of hunger and high food prices. The grain and goods Philip seized brought him a windfall of seven hundred talents, and timber from the captured ships went to the manufacture of more siege weapons.

At last Philip had committed an overt act of war, something he could not explain away – although he made a lame attempt – and the Philippizers in Athens could not excuse. Demosthenes, reflecting back on this moment, saw it as a definitive break. "I tell you, that man" – Philip – "dissolved the peace when he seized the cargo ships," he said in reply to Aeschines, who had accused *him* of warmongering.[8]

On Demosthenes' advice, the Assembly ordered the stone tablet displaying the Peace of Philocrates to be smashed. The treaty was thus formally abrogated. Athens and Philip were once again at war.

What occurred in the year that followed is known largely through speeches of Demosthenes and Aeschines, but since these were delivered to sway a jury, neither account can be taken on trust. The basic course of events by which Philip once again entered central Greece is clear enough. The sequence began with a shift of allegiance in which Philip lost a crucial base of Hellenic support, that of Thebes.

Up to this point the Thebans had been allied with Philip under the terms of a treaty. Philip had spent several years in Thebes in his teens before his accession; he had learned much from watching the Theban land army in action, lessons he later used in his role as Macedon's king. The two nations had many interests in common and had fought on the same side in the Sacred War. But Thebes was unhappy about the way Philip ended that war — his decision not to destroy the Phocians — and shared with Athens a growing unease over Philip's encroachment on central Greece. In 339, despite their alliance with Philip, the Thebans seized several forts at the south end of the pass of Thermopylae, kicking out the Thessalians who guarded them. Their move declared that they, like the Athenians, mistrusted Philip and wanted the option of keeping him out of the region.

The Thebans had reason to fear that Philip would move south again, as he had in 346. For at about this time, new troubles broke out involving the shrine of Delphi. Demosthenes thought that Philip engineered them using Aeschines as his agent, and some modern scholars suspect he was right about that. All we can say for certain is that some sort of secret dealings led to the start of a *Fourth* Sacred War, only a few years after the Third had ended.

The conflagration began with a tiny spark. Aeschines, serving as spokesman for Athens at a meeting of the Amphictyons, raised the point that the residents of Amphissa, a town in the Delphic plain, had been farming lands that were set aside for Apollo. The Amphictyons went in person to confront the trespassers, and in the fight that erupted blood was shed on both sides. A larger Amphictyonic meeting was called to discuss the problem, and sacred war was declared against Amphissa. Neither Thebes nor Athens took part in that meeting; both states were loath to choose sides once again in a sacred war, perhaps for fear they would end up on different ones.

Command of the Amphictyonic forces was given to a Thessalian, who promptly brought Amphissa to heel. But as soon as his army departed, Amphissa reneged on its promise and defied the council again. By this time Philip was back in Macedon, having completed a long campaign in lands to his north. On the motion of the Thessalians, the Amphictyons appointed Philip, the savior of Delphi six years earlier, to conduct the new Sacred War and ensure that Amphissa paid a price for its hubris. For the second time, Philip received carte blanche to enter central Greece with his army—if, that is, the Thebans allowed him to pass.

Things had played out very much to Philip's advantage, leading Demosthenes to claim a conspiracy. "Do not go about saying, Athenians, that Greece suffered these things at the hands of one man," he later told a crowd of jurors, referring to Philip. "Earth and gods above! It was not through one man, but through many wicked people in various cities." The leader of the conspirators, Demosthenes argued, was Aeschines, who first set in motion the whole twisted sequence. He denounced Aeschines as an *aliterion*, a mythical spirit of vengeance and destruction.[9] (We shall come soon to the speech in which he leveled these charges, "On the Crown," his rhetorical magnum opus.)

Because Thebes held the forts at Thermopylae, both Thebes and Athens assumed that Philip could still be kept out of their region, whatever the Amphictyons might decree. But that narrow chokepoint was not, as it happened, the only route south for an army. A rougher but passable mountain track allowed Philip to sidestep the Thebans and bring his troops into the province of Doris, as though to attack Amphissa. His swerve came as a surprise to the Greeks, but a bigger shock was to follow. Instead of heading south toward his official objective, Philip turned east. In a sudden swoop he seized Elateia, a city astride the road that led toward Thebes and, ultimately, toward Athens.

Demosthenes recounted years later the moment at which Athenians learned of this move. It was evening when the news was brought to the *prytaneis*, the fifty Boule members who formed its executive board; the men were then taking their evening meal in the council house. They instantly rose from their dinner and set in motion measures for calling an emergency Assembly the following morning. Wicker stalls in the marketplace were set on fire, presumably as a signal to the whole citizenry, and trumpets were blown. An excited murmur spread through Athens as news of Philip's aggression hit home. From Elateia, Athenians knew, only a few days' march could bring Philip's fearsome siege engines up to their walls.

At the next day's Assembly session, Demosthenes later recounted, a crier put the question, "Who wishes to speak?" The call was repeated several more times, but no one came forward. Finally Demosthenes stepped to the bema, taking upon himself the burden of the rescue of Athens. "I alone, of the speakers and politicians, did not desert my place in the ranks of service, amid great perils," he boasted in this later account, no doubt truthfully—for those whom he addressed would have remembered this moment well enough to detect a lie.[10]

From the bema Demosthenes interpreted Philip's movements in Phocis, near the Boeotian border, as a way to shore up relations with Thebes. "What does he want, and why did he take Elateia? He wants, by showing his power and stationing arms near [Thebes], to encourage his friends and give them heart, and to strike terror into his enemies, so that they will either take fright and yield or be forced to do so."[11] The Philippizers in Thebes, recently on the defensive, might now be emboldened and take the policy reins. The result of a stronger alliance, Demosthenes pointed out, might be a joint operation in which Thebes and Philip would invade Athenian territory. Invoking this threat was more than mere fearmongering, for Philip was at that moment sending envoys to Thebes; among the plans these speakers were bringing was a combined attack of exactly this kind.

Demosthenes was aware of the anti-Theban bias in the Assembly, born of decades of strife, yet he urged his hearers to look past their grudges. "If we choose in the present circumstance to call to mind any harsh thing done to us by the Thebans . . . we'll bring to pass just what Philip would pray for," he said.[12] Though recently on opposing sides in the Third Sacred War, Athens and Thebes had a common enemy now, and a reason to work together. Demosthenes proposed that an armed force march to Eleusis, near Attica's border with Boeotia, to show the Thebans a steely resolve, and that a team of ten envoys be sent to Thebes to argue for an alliance.

Demosthenes stepped down from the bema and waited for a reaction. According to his later account, "everyone approved and no one said anything in opposition," though many in the crowd that day would have preferred to ally with Philip, not Thebes.[13] The heated emotions in the Assembly made it hard for dissenters to declare themselves in a show-of-hands vote. Unanimous or not, the proposal was passed, and Demosthenes was appointed to head the diplomatic team, which included his ally Hyperides. With Theban allegiance teetering in the balance, Demosthenes left for Boeotia — the most crucial rhetorical mission he had yet undertaken.

Philip's ambassadors were already on the scene in Thebes when Demosthenes arrived for the crucial Assembly debate. The Macedonian envoys spoke first and made a convincing case. The Thebans were welcome to join with Philip, they said, in invading Athenian land; if this seemed distasteful, Thebes might simply stay neutral and let Philip march through Boeotia, as well as return the Thermopylae forts to Philip's Thessalian allies. For those small concessions the Thebans would be allowed to plunder the Attic countryside. Flocks of herd animals, slaves, and timber pillaged from houses would all be theirs for the taking. However, if they refused to grant Philip safe passage, the envoys made clear that the Thebans themselves would come under attack.

We will probably never know how Demosthenes countered this offer, though his speech was judged a masterpiece. Demosthenes himself later told the Athenian demos "I'd give my entire life" to recount the details of that address, yet he somehow declined to do so.[14] The omission is striking, given how often Demosthenes rehashes his political triumphs. We can guess that later events made it prudent not to dwell on the mission to Thebes. Partly due to Demosthenes' interventions, Thebes was shortly to suffer as few Greek cities had suffered. The memory of the great anti-Philip alliance was to become a source of deep pain.

The choice of allegiance, Athens or Philip, must not have been easy for Thebes, but Demosthenes offered the Thebans incredibly generous terms. Athens would pay two-thirds of the cost of the coming war, he told their Assembly, but allow Thebes an equal share of command. Demosthenes was later attacked by Aeschines for "stealing the council house and the democracy out of Athens and transferring them to the Theban Cadmeia," a vivid way of saying he had given away the store. An even greater concession Demosthenes offered was recognition by Athens of the Boeotian League, the federation from which Thebes drew much of its power. Athens had for decades refused to legitimize the league, but Demosthenes felt that this was no time to hold back. "Pay close attention to this point," he had told the Assembly at Athens: "Don't ask for a thing from the Thebans, for that would be shameful in this critical moment."[15]

The Thebans made their choice and sided with Athens. As the Athenians had done with the Peace of Philocrates, they smashed up the stone on which their treaty with Philip had been inscribed, declaring themselves at war. Some no doubt had been swayed by "the power of the orator," as a contemporary historian wrote, "which kindled their courage and enflamed their love of honor"; some lacked faith that Philip would keep his word. A source that has recently come to light, a long-lost speech by Hyperides recovered thanks to modern technologies, indicates that Demosthenes had not, in fact, won Thebes over by his address; the alliance with Athens was finalized only months later.[16] Of course, Hyperides, like all politicians, had his own ax to grind.

Whenever the decision was made, Demosthenes got what he wanted, a Thebes–Athens axis committed to driving Philip out of central Greece. He promptly set out to visit other cities to win more allies. According to Aeschines, he became so zealous in this pursuit that he told the Assembly he would go as envoy wherever he wished, even without formal approval. Demosthenes described events differently, claiming that he had shown unique energy by first proposing the dispatch of envoys and then going on those missions himself.[17] He reported having won commitments from Megara, Corinth, Euboea, and Corcyra, among other places.

The coalition taking the field against Philip was going to be huge, more than thirty thousand infantry and thousands more cavalry, the largest Greek force assembled in decades. Its member states added to it by hiring a squad of ten thousand mercenaries, which they sent north to block the road to Amphissa. They meant to bar Philip from once again making himself the champion of Apollo. Meanwhile the Athenian army moved into Boeotia, a region with broad, level plains well suited for phalanx combat – "the dancing floor of Ares," as Epaminondas, the great Theban leader, had termed it.[18]

Demosthenes joined that army and prepared to fight as a hoplite, an infantry soldier. Despite his weak constitution and lack of combat experience, at age forty-six, at the height of his political sway, he brought out his spear and his armor and made ready to march to Boeotia. On his shield was painted the legend AGATHEI TYCHEI, "with good fortune" – expressing the hope that the good luck he claimed as his special asset would accompany him, and his city, into the coming battle. Athens would need that luck, for skill, training, weaponry, and tactics were all on the side of Philip and Macedon.

CHAPTER SEVEN

Demosthenes of Paeania,
Son of Demosthenes, Proposes . . .

D emosthenes was married at the time the Peace of Philocrates was dissolved, and father to a daughter, but we know
next to nothing about his family life. He never mentioned his wife
and children—he later had two sons by his wife and, reportedly,
one by a courtesan—in his extant orations, though he apparently
did so in a now-lost speech with the unusual title "On the Gold."
We do not even know the name of Demosthenes' wife, although we
do know the name of a mistress to whom he was linked, the famously beautiful Laïs. A historical writer of the early third century
BCE, Idomeneus of Lampsacus, reported in a now-lost work that
Demosthenes was "unbridled regarding sex," but this may only reflect mudslinging gossip. Aeschines certainly heaped on the mud by
harping on the Batalus theme, the idea that Demosthenes favored
male partners and played a passive role more suited to women.[1]

Demosthenes' sons seem not to have followed in their father's
career footsteps, or at least they left no mark on Athenian politics.
A nephew, Demochares, however, the son of his sister, was des-

tined for a long and important career at the bema. The boy must have been old enough by the early 330s to show he had his uncle's speechmaking skills; perhaps Demosthenes helped him develop them, though he often discouraged young people from entering public life. "If two roads had been laid out for me in my youth," he is said to have told a group of would-be protégés, "one leading to the bema and the Assembly, the other straight on to doom, and if I had chanced to know in advance the evils connected to politics – the fears, the rivalries, the slanders, the struggles – I'd have set out on the road that leads toward death."[2]

In the critical years 339 and 338, the road that Demosthenes followed led into Boeotia, the homeland of Thebes. It seems he had mapped out that route long before, given that Aeschines, in 343, accused him of "Boeotizing." He kept his plans quiet, however, in recognition of the dislike that most Athenians felt for the Thebans, playing down his pro-Theban leanings in speeches and maintaining a low profile as proxenos, or agent, of Thebes, a post in which he advocated for Theban interests in Athens. He then waited until the time came, when Philip seized Elateia, to argue that the best hopes of Athens lay in alliance with Thebes; at that point, it seemed, there was no alternative.

The Thebans had proven their skill in land warfare some three decades earlier by defeating the Spartans, who until that time had been masters of every infantry engagement. The Thebans had hurled at the Spartans their Sacred Band, a unique elite corps made up of pairs of male lovers; the principle was that a man in love would do anything to defend his beloved and demonstrate courage before him. They had also used new approaches to phalanx tactics, placing a deeper block of fighters on their left wing, facing their enemy's strong point, and thinning their right. But the generals who had devised these approaches, Pelopidas and Epaminondas, were long gone, and those who had taken their places were less innovative. The Sacred Band was still in arms, but its recent achievements were few. Strategy had evolved for the Greeks in the fourth century, but their infantry gear, the *hopla* for which their hoplites were named, had not changed over the centuries. In every Greek city, those who could afford to do so maintained a heavy wooden shield, a seven- or eight-foot thrusting spear, a metal helmet, perhaps a set of greaves, and a cuirass or thick linen corslet. The armor and shield afforded near-total protection so long as the phalanx kept in formation, with shields of the frontline men joined together to form a defensive wall. Shields, spears, and helmets varied only slightly from city to city and even less over time; each hoplite owned his own set, and making changes required new outlays of funds.

In Macedon, by contrast, the kit of the infantryman was evolving dramatically in this era, due largely to Philip. He had introduced a spear, the *sarisa,* more than twice as long as that of the Greeks. Its length and weight required the use of both hands, so the Macedonian shield had been reduced in size to enable it to be hung from a soldier's neck. Philip had shifted strategy away from protection and toward a more vigorous, penetrating attack on the theory that a strong offense reduced the need for defense. The king paid for this gear out of royal funds and issued it to his troops, creating, in modern terms, a professional army, as opposed to a citizen militia.

Demosthenes recognized that Philip had altered the face of land warfare, but he failed to perceive the importance of the new Macedonian weapons. In a passage of his "Third Philippic," he warned Athenians about the forces that Philip was leading: "Philip goes wherever he wants, not by bringing up his phalanx, but by furnishing himself with light-armed troops, cavalrymen, archers, mercenaries, and that sort of power."[3] He made it appear that Philip was fighting dirty, using hired troops and auxiliaries rather than meeting his foes in open, hand-to-hand combat. Either Demosthenes' informants had not told him about the sarisa and the tough recruits who wielded it, or else he concealed the news from Athenians. They would learn the truth soon enough.

Other observations in the "Third Philippic" are more astute. Demosthenes noted that "there's no difference between summer and winter" to Philip, no season at which he took a pause from campaigning, as Greek armies did. Philip kept troops in service year-round, unlike the city-state forces he faced, which were made up largely of farmers whose fields, at some point, needed tending. Although the Spartans had paved the way in breaking free of the calendar by having their serfs grow their food, even they, as Demosthenes observed, went home from the front in wintertime, when forage was scarce and supplies would have to be bought. Demosthenes made the case in the "Third Philippic" that by staying in the field year-round, Philip was relying on cash, not crops, and trampling on hallowed traditions.

Philip confirmed Demosthenes' words by keeping his army encamped in Boeotia during the winter of 339–338. Two small engagements were fought in those months between Philip's forces and the Greek coalition, but little is known about them. A more consequential action took place farther south, on the road to Amphissa. The ten thousand mercenaries Athens had hired, at great expense, were blocking Philip's path toward the town and holding a strong position. But Philip dislodged them by means of a clever ruse. He sent a letter addressed to one of his staff explaining that he was leaving the region to deal with matters in Thrace, then made sure it was intercepted. Thinking that Philip was gone, the mercenaries abandoned their stronghold. Philip marched through to Amphissa unchallenged; the soldiers he had tricked, now outflanked, dispersed and departed.

Athens had lost an expensive asset and suffered a blow to morale. Nonetheless Athenians felt they had chosen the right path — the path of confrontation. At the Dionysia festival in March 338, yet another gold crown was presented to Demosthenes, awarded on the motion of Hyperides and one of his allies. With this highly public acclaim, the city declared that it stood behind its alliance with Thebes, and the war.

And yet the Athenians kept seeing omens that showed, as Aeschines later insisted, that the gods were trying to warn them, "all but talking to us in human voices." One day as initiates washed themselves in the sea in preparation for sacred rites that took place at Eleusis, some were attacked by sharks. A seer urged that the Delphic oracle be consulted as to the meaning of the attack, but Demosthenes stood in the way of the motion, claiming that "the Pythian priestess is Philippizing."[4] He reminded Athens of the words of Epaminondas, the great Theban leader, who just before a climactic battle had told his troops to ignore all such portents: *One omen only is best, to fight for one's homeland,*" Epaminondas had said, quoting Homer.[5] The Thebans had followed his dictum, and won.

Among those in Athens who worried about the war was Phocion, the cautious statesman who had served his city for decades as strategos (general). In a testy exchange in the Assembly, he spoke against Demosthenes, who was urging the city to carry the war to Boeotia rather than await an attack nearer home. "My good fellow," said Phocion, with ironic hauteur, "let's not deliberate where we are to fight, but how we are to win."[6] No matter where the battle took place, if Athens lost — as he feared it would do — the war would arrive on the city's doorstep soon enough.

Not only Phocion and his faction had doubts about the coming battle; Philip too felt uncertain, and he reached out to Athens and Thebes in a last-ditch attempt at negotiation. He hoped to avoid a clash in which so much was at risk. Demosthenes, though, opposed any change of course; he wanted a showdown. According to Aeschines, he swore a great oath before the Assembly, calling on the goddess Athena as witness, that he would grab by the hair any man who spoke up for peace and haul him away for imprisonment.[7] Aeschines claims that Demosthenes also shamed the Thebans, calling them traitors to Greece, when *they* seemed to waver, forcing them to stay the course. However things worked out, it was clear to the faction Demosthenes headed, now with the help of Hyperides, that an opportune moment for action could not be let slip. Athens had waited a long time – perhaps *too* long – before standing up to Philip with all its strength; if it did not press the fight now, it might never do so.

By the summer of 338 all diplomatic efforts had arrived at dead ends. The two coalitions – Philip's Macedonians with their Greek allies, especially the Thessalians, against the Theban-Athenian axis with *its* allies – prepared for a major set battle, one of the largest ever, with nearly seventy thousand fighters taking part.

Deployment of huge land armies in phalanx lines more than a mile long required a broad, open plain. Following the conventions of war, both combatants made their way to a spot of this kind, then arranged their divisions at leisure on opposite sides of the field. The site they selected was a plain outside the city of Chaeronea. The Greeks had a slight numerical edge, but their forces were far less seasoned; Philip's troops had been in almost continuous action for years. Many Athenians, including Demosthenes, had never before fought a major land battle, and none had faced the next-generation weapon, the sarisa, that Philip had introduced. The first sight they had of a phalanx that bristled with these fearsome lances must have been deeply unsettling.

In typical fashion, both armies placed their strongest troops on the right wing, facing the weaker left of their foe. Philip's unit anchored the Macedonian right, squaring off against the Athenians. On the opposite end of the field, the Thebans, with their formidable Sacred Band, held the right flank of the Greek coalition, facing a new and untried Macedonian leader, a youth only sixteen years old: Philip's son Alexander, entrusted now, in his first combat role, with the task of dealing with Thebes. We do not know whether Alexander, soon to be known as "the Great," was leading a unit of cavalry, as in his subsequent clashes, or whether he fought the Thebans on foot, toe to toe. In either case, his part was to be decisive.

The battle was hard-fought and bloody. It is possible that (as one source reports) Philip tricked the Athenians by feigning retreat and drawing them out of position.[8] Such a move would have made sense, since Athens and Thebes had not fought together in a single formation until recent months; an opponent would naturally try to break the two allies apart. Philip's troops were more cohesive and better practiced at keeping their ranks united, an essential skill in infantry combat. These seasoned Macedonians laid into their foes with devastating effect, leaving a thousand Athenians dead and putting the others to rout.

On the opposite side of the plain, Alexander broke through the Thebans' line and demolished their Sacred Band. These 300 men, 150 male couples, had been the backbone of Theban strength ever since their unit was formed, forty years earlier. Their mass grave, discovered at Chaeronea in 1880, gives evidence of how they suffered in death. Arms and legs were slashed to the bone, and skulls were pierced by the fearsome spikes that tipped the sarisa's butt end. Two hundred and fifty-four skeletons were found in that grave, so either some of the unit escaped with their lives or else their bodies were too mangled in death to be identified later as members of the elite cohort. Many other Thebans were slain in the battle as well, their numbers unrecorded in our sources.

And what of Demosthenes? He survived Chaeronea, unhurt in body but soon to be gravely wounded in reputation. Aeschines claimed he "deserted his station," that is, broke formation and left his comrades exposed to harm. Other political enemies painted a more damning picture: Demosthenes, they said, had thrown away his shield as he ran, so fearful that when his trailing cloak caught on a branch, he turned around, thinking a pursuer had snagged it, and started to beg for his life. Of course, a charge of cowardice, like that of sexual deviancy, provided a powerful political weapon, so we do well to view these stories with skepticism. No doubt Demosthenes *did* run from battle, along with thousands of others; anyone who survived the collapse of a phalanx *had* to have run at some point.

The Athenian escapees collected themselves on a nearby hill and sent a message to Philip, seeking a truce to pick up their dead – a formal admission that they had lost and Philip had won. But Philip did not grant this time-honored concession. He retained and cremated the thousand corpses; he also, for the moment, held on to his two thousand Athenian captives, in hopes of bringing a quick end to the war. A siege of Athens, if he were forced to conduct one, would be protracted and messy, and would likely result in a lasting estrangement between Macedon and Athens. As things stood, he had hopes of detente with the Greek world's foremost naval power; he would need its help very soon.

A legend recounted by Plutarch tells that, in the aftermath of his victory, Philip got drunk and wandered among the Greek dead, chanting a mocking phrase: "Demosthenes of Paeania, son of Demosthenes, proposes . . . ," the formula with which Demosthenes moved his Assembly decrees. Philip gave the words metrical stress as though they belonged to a comic play, to better belittle his beaten antagonist.[9] The anecdote may be apocryphal, but it speaks to the disillusionment many Athenians felt in the wake of the battle. Their system of governance, exemplified by Demosthenes' oratory and the sovereign Assembly, had been bested by a warrior-autocrat. Philip had cut through their wordy political culture as easily as his son would later cut through the Gordian knot.

A second legend, or perhaps an extension of the first one, relates that Philip conducted a drunken revel amid the Athenian slain, exulting at the misfortunes of his foes. An Athenian prisoner, Demades, witnessed the spectacle and spoke reproachfully to the king. Philip took the man's point, sobered up, and regained his composure. Then he deputized Demades to be his envoy to the people of Athens, appointing him to carry the terms of surrender. This story too may be invented, but Demades *did* serve as go-between, then and for years to come, as Athens and Macedon worked out their new relations. Trusted by Philip, he filled a diplomatic slot left vacant by Demosthenes, who for a long time had been persona non grata in Pella.

To help ensure that the offer Demades carried received a favorable hearing in Athens, Philip sent back the ashes of the Athenian dead in an honorific procession led by Alexander. He also returned his Athenian prisoners of war without demanding ransom, an extraordinary act of clemency. He was hoping for a rapprochement, despite all the blood he had shed. His terms of surrender were mild: he would not force Athens to give up democracy, nor would he install a garrison—two measures that Sparta, much earlier, had taken after defeating Athens in the Peloponnesian War. Philip would let the proud city keep its traditions, even while forcing Thebes to accept both a garrison force and an oligarchic government led by his puppets.

The Athenians were hugely relieved when they learned of Philip's terms. Fears had been running high once again that the city would need to stand a siege; Hyperides had even proposed that slaves be set free and foreign residents of Athens be given citizenship in order to swell the ranks of armed forces. When the panic had passed, Assembly speakers had pointed out that such measures were unconstitutional, and Hyperides had been forced to defend himself. "The weapons of Macedon blinded my sight," he declared; "not I, but the battle of Chaeronea, proposed that decree."[10] His lame self-justifications must have sufficed, for we hear of no consequences.

Demades, together with Phocion and Aeschines, led the city's negotiations with Philip and worked out a settlement. Athens would join a treaty organization that Philip was forming with nearly all the Greek city-states, a kind of United Hellas under Macedonian leadership. In the new world now taking shape, the Greeks would make common decisions at Corinth, the league's meeting place, and Philip would translate those decisions into action. Everything the league passed would have to accord with Philip's designs, for its constituent states were largely under his power. Sparta, alone of the mainland Greek cities, stayed out of the league, deeming (correctly) that Philip would not extend himself so far south or challenge such a formidable fighting force.

Demosthenes, as far as we know, did not stand in the way of the League of Corinth (as it has come to be called), even though the arrangement codified the power of Macedon. He was busy fending off indictments brought by those who blamed him for Chaeronea. These indictments, he later claimed, were lodged by his foes at the rate of one per day, yet none ever made headway.[11] Athens chose not to put him on trial, as the citizenry would have done had it wanted to jettison him as a leader. In other cases where politicians had placed bad bets, or generals had lost battles, the demos had vented its anger with banishments, fines, even death sentences. No such fates befell Demosthenes — at least, not immediately.

Far from being punished for failure, Demosthenes was awarded a high civic honor. After Philip's return of their dead, it fell to the Athenians, as always on such occasions, to choose someone to deliver a eulogy. The solemn rite of the funeral oration was immortalized by Thucydides, reporting on the occasion, nearly a century earlier, when Pericles gave the address. Ten cypress-wood coffins were carried by wagons to the cemetery, one for each of Athens's ten tribes, containing the ashes of that tribe's dead; then a cenotaph was brought in for the soldiers whose bodies had not been recovered. The city's chosen speaker delivered his words to crowds of families and friends, giving expression to their grief and searching for meaning in the deaths of their loved ones. In the aftermath of Chaeronea, Athens chose Demosthenes for this role.

To judge by surviving examples, Athenian funeral speeches had highly conventional themes: the glories of the city's mythic past and its historical greatness; the noble natures of those who had given their lives; the immortal fame of the dead and the comfort it might bring their families. Those themes were perhaps still fresh when Pericles had expressed them, or at least he had given them life. Demosthenes could not pull off the same feat. Much of his speech, it must be said, remains trapped in timeworn formulas, so much so that some modern scholars think that it is not his work but a later rhetorical exercise by an impersonator. This theory would be plausible were it not for the petty, but authentically Demosthenic, way in which the speech addresses the recent defeat.

In the midst of exalting the dead, Demosthenes could not resist a reminder that *he* had urged confronting Philip long before Chaeronea, but no one had listened. "Though there was much folly, mixed with baseness, among the Greek states, at a time when these things could have been prevented without running risks — a folly that failed to foresee some dangers and pretended not to see others — nonetheless these men," he proclaimed, indicating the dead, "did not bear ill-will, but stepped forward and eagerly offered their all."[12] His grim implication was that if the Greeks had followed his counsel and stopped Philip sooner, no one need have died.

That passage strikes an unfortunate, self-righteous note, but there is worse to come. Though generally the speech blames *tyche*, luck or chance, for the loss of the battle, at one point it turns to more personal causes. "If anyone sees fit to level a charge for these things," Demosthenes said, referring to Chaeronea, "someone might with reason find fault with the Thebans who were in command." Though given worthy troops to work with, these Theban generals "did not make good use of any of them."[13] The voice of the eulogist here gives way to that of the politician, whose goal is to shift the onus of failure onto the shoulders of others.

Demosthenes did not mention Philip by name in the speech, referring more vaguely to "the master of our opponents." He made the case that the bravery of the Athenians at Chaeronea had, in the end, accomplished a valuable goal, deterring Philip from an attack on Athens and forcing him into his later conciliations. Demosthenes refrained from comment on the new treaty arrangements, but he did note gloomily at one point that with the passing of the war dead the Greeks had lost their *axioma*, their reason for feeling self-worth. It was as though the light of day had vanished, leaving all of life a wearisome, difficult toil.[14] This vision of a joyless future left little room for hope in the newly formed League of Corinth.

Nearing the end of the speech, Demosthenes struck a Periclean note, depicting the virtues of the dead as products of Athenian democracy—though not for the reasons Pericles had expressed. In a democratic system, Demosthenes explained, all people have freedom of speech, so anyone, high or low, can attack a shirker or coward. Such public shaming motivates soldiers to do their best in the field. In oligarchies, by contrast, citizens fight out of fear, not shame, and if they fight poorly, they can appease their masters with bribes in order to wipe clean their reputation.[15] This is a strange argument, which holds out public reproach rather than patriotism as the primary factor that spurs men to bravery. Perhaps it was partly inspired by the reproach Demosthenes himself was then under for having deserted his station—a charge that was to dog him the rest of his life.

Athens chose Demosthenes as its funeral orator based on his eloquence, but the assignment clearly did not suit his temperament. The solemn tone of elegy was not his natural voice; it did not allow him to draw on his anger, his outrage, or his sarcastic wit, the fuels that powered his rhetoric. He was at his best when combating an adversary, a Philip or an Aeschines, but amid the communal grief of a public interment he had no such foil. Even so, he managed indirect hits at those who were starting to blame him for Chaeronea. He made clear that Athens should have confronted Philip far earlier than it did; that bad luck, not bad strategy, had brought the Greeks low; and, in his least attractive moment, that the coalition had been poorly led by the Thebans. It was he, we recall, who had insisted on giving Thebes joint command of the troops.

Guided now by Phocion and other accommodationists, Athens joined the body that Philip had founded, the League of Corinth. Member states pledged to respect one another's territory, to vote on common policies, and to make Philip the guarantor of their safety and enforcer of their will. They agreed to contribute troops and ships to augment Philip's forces—a provision that caused a flurry of anger in Athens but in the end was accepted.

Philip had welded the Greek city-states—all but recalcitrant Sparta—into a federation, the goal that Isocrates, now nearly a hundred years old, had urged in his writings. In his last surviving treatise, an open letter to Philip written just after Chaeronea, Isocrates hailed the Macedonian king as the savior of Hellas. Philip's mission now, Isocrates wrote, was to lead a crusade into Asia, to bring to heel "the king who is now called Great." "For then," Isocrates promised, "there will be nothing left for you except to become a god."[16]

Philip was planning to do exactly those things, but fate intervened.

CHAPTER EIGHT

He Always Says and Does
What Is Best for the Demos

In the period following Chaeronea, Demosthenes kept a low
profile in the Assembly. Plutarch records that he no longer put
his name on legal motions but used his shills to advance them
under their own names; evidently his sponsorship was no longer
an asset. The leading voice in the city was now that of Demades,
who had gone as envoy to deal with Philip and had brought back
favorable terms. Another orator of the day, Pytheas, noted the contrasting lifestyles of the two leading speakers, one rising, the other
declining: where Demosthenes abstained from wine and worked
on his speeches late into the night, Demades got drunk every day,
lived for sensual pleasures, and came to be recognized by his prodigious potbelly.[1]

The new political landscape favored Philippizers, including an
aggressive upstart by the name of Diondas. Determined to punish
the anti-Philip faction, Diondas filed one legal action after another
against its members, accruing fifty by the time he was twenty-five.
By one account he filed three suits against Hyperides in a single day.

His enemies saw him as a typical *sycophant*, the word the Athenians coined for those who were paid for filing suits on others' behalf or who extorted money from those they indicted. In the Athenian legal system, where even the lowly could initiate suits without bureaucratic procedures whenever a chance presented itself, such opportunists proliferated and were scorned in the same way as modern ambulance-chasing lawyers.

Diondas's most serious action was the *graphe paranomon*, an indictment for proposing an illegal motion, that he brought against Hyperides. He charged that the orator's motion in 338 to award a gold crown to Demosthenes was contrary to the law. This move was imbued with political meaning, for both its targets had pushed for the war against Philip. In the wake of the Chaeronea defeat, the pro-Philip faction saw a chance to score points with the public by finding scapegoats; Diondas's lawsuit targeted two choice ones. But the suit stayed on hold, without moving forward to trial.

Diondas was so eager to Philippize that he volunteered to go north when, under the new treaty's terms, Philip requested soldiers and ships from Athens. Philip's army was massing for an invasion of Asia, a project that had been approved by the Greek states meeting at Corinth but that was, in essence, a Macedonian mission. Philip gathered recruits from many Greek cities, both to expand his armed forces and to stop those cities from contemplating rebellion; effectively, the recruits he levied became hostages. From Athens, where rebellion was not unlikely, Philip took six hundred hoplites, perhaps including Diondas, and sixty cavalrymen.

The levy that Demosthenes had worked to prevent at the time of the Peace of Philocrates, and that Athens had staunchly resisted, had at last taken place. Athenians were grieved by this new subjection and thought of refusing, but Phocion, whose fortunes had also risen with Philip's, convinced them to fill the request. His foreign policy, based on his long military command, was summed up in the advice he once gave the Assembly: "Either be foremost in strength of arms, or be friends with those who are foremost."[2] That strategy meant doing what Philip asked, at least in the short term.

Demosthenes had been thrust out of leadership, but he still had supporters in Athens who sought to repair his image. A service he performed in 337, the year after Chaeronea, gave them an opening. He had been appointed to oversee the upkeep of the Athenian walls, and was given state funds to do so, but when the money fell short he added a meaningful sum from his own fortune. That gesture, plus a stint in a financial oversight role, prompted an ally, Ctesiphon, to propose yet another gold crown for Demosthenes, "because he always says and does what is best for the demos." The motion's wording focused attention on what Demosthenes had done *right*, in preference to the failure of Chaeronea.

Ctesiphon's motion easily passed the Boule (council) and was headed for the Assembly, but then an old foe, Aeschines, stepped forward to block it. Unwilling to see Demosthenes rehabilitated, Aeschines too brought a suit of graphe paranomon. He accused Ctesiphon of an illegal motion, thus rejecting the claim that Demosthenes had spoken and acted in the best interest of Athens. The feud that had started nearly ten years before, in the conflict over the Peace of Philocrates, was heating up once again.

Twice in two years, Demosthenes' friends had gotten motions passed to award him crowns, and both times his enemies had intervened. Athens awaited two major trials in which the questions of Chaeronea, and of the entire conflict with Philip, might finally be answered. Had Demosthenes guided the city wisely, with good intentions, or had he ruined Athenian power, and much of Greece as well, through incompetence, malfeasance, or corruption? Should he still play a leadership role in the era to come?

Before either trial could begin, news arrived that made both moot and overturned the entire political order. Philip had been assassinated. His son Alexander, barely twenty years old, had taken his place.

The deed had been carried out by one of Philip's cadets in the midst of a procession to honor a royal wedding. The perpetrator was killed by guards before being questioned, hence no one knew whether he had acted alone; conspiracy rumors were rife. But the mystery of the murder was overshadowed, in Athenian minds, by more immediate questions: Had they regained their freedom? Was the treaty they signed, committing themselves to the League of Corinth, still in effect? Was the invasion of Asia still going forward, and if so, did Athens still need to participate? Could Alexander, who had proven his prowess in battle but not on a throne, hold his father's empire together?

Demosthenes saw only good things for Athens, and for himself, in this sudden turn of events. He had been the first in the city to get the news, owing to a message dispatched by an ally in Macedon. According to Aeschines, he used his advance knowledge to win new repute as a public benefactor. He came before the Boule, Aeschines claimed, and told the governing council that he had had a significant dream: the city's protectors, Zeus and Athena, had told him of Philip's death. When the news later broke more widely, it appeared as though the gods had chosen him as their messenger.[3] It's unclear whether Demosthenes actually did this, or, if he did, how Aeschines knew that the report of the dream had been a ruse.

Demosthenes was at the time in mourning for his daughter, who had died a few days before Philip's assassination. He was wearing funereal black, as was customary, but when news came of Philip's death, he donned a festive white cloak and a garland in order to carry out a sacrifice to the gods. For this change of garments, Aeschines took him to task, implying he had shown himself to be a bad father and therefore could never be a good leader. Centuries after Aeschines mounted his charge, Plutarch assailed him for it. In his Life of Demosthenes, Plutarch saw a valuable lesson in the change of clothing: public and statesmanlike duties must outweigh private griefs. Aeschines' words to the contrary, wrote Plutarch, were doing great harm, softening those who read them and leaving them less equipped for demands of office.[4] As often in his *Parallel Lives,* Plutarch tried to see the best in his subject and reject criticism.

Much of Athens felt, as Demosthenes did, that the news of Philip's death deserved celebration. Many people donned garlands and carried out sacrifices. The Assembly seemed in favor of such displays, but when a motion to make them official came up for debate, Phocion rose to oppose it. Rejoicing over the death of an ally, he said – perhaps with a glance at Demosthenes – was highly unseemly. "Besides," he added, "the force that was ranged against you at Chaeronea has been diminished by only a single person."[5] Ever the realist in foreign relations, he felt that Athens was still no match for Macedon if it came to another fight.

No one knew what to expect from Alexander, the monarch who would now determine Greece's future. Athenians had seen the young man in two very different roles, once on the field of Chaeronea, then, shortly afterward, in their own streets, when he led the procession escorting the city's war dead. He had shown himself highly adept both times, but Demosthenes – now speaking boldly again in Assembly meetings – called him a "boy" and compared him to Margites, an oafish figure from literature. He claimed that Alexander would not have the guts to control a vast empire but would stay at home in Pella, playing it safe and reading the entrails of sacri-fices.[6] Alexander soon proved otherwise by having the federation at Corinth affirm the invasion of Asia and appoint him to head it. He seemed to want to pick up right where Philip left off.

Demosthenes was doing his best to prevent that. By this time he had a network of partisans extending all across the Aegean world. He started dispatching letters to correspondents, seeking to get Alexander blocked or even overthrown. He wrote to Attalus, a Macedonian general who hated Alexander, urging him to mount a coup; before Attalus could act, however, Alexander had him mur-dered. Other letters passed back and forth between Demosthenes and Persian officials in Asia. These agents of the Great King—no longer Artaxerxes III, but his newly installed successor Darius III— were worried about the invasion and willing to funnel money to those who could stop it. Demosthenes served as a conduit for their cash, some of which may have stuck to his fingers (a question to be explored in due course).

The most consequential outreach Demosthenes made was to Thebes, the city with which he had forged close ties. Thebes had been under the Macedonian boot for the past two years, garrisoned by a contingent of troops and governed by a junta of Philip's pup-pets. Demosthenes kept in contact with Thebans who hated Mace-don's power, both those in Thebes and others who had been kicked out and were living in exile in Athens. A revolt led by these insur-gents, he felt, could spark a wider rebellion in which the old, anti-Macedon coalition would quickly re-form. Athens could again take its place beside Thebes to champion Greek liberty, but this time it would prevail. The failure of Chaeronea could be redeemed.

In the summer of 335, when Alexander had been in power the better part of a year, the moment for such a revolt seemed at hand. Alexander was far away in the north, fighting rebellious Balkan tribes, when a rumor reached Athens that he had been killed in battle. Demosthenes went before the Assembly and produced a man who claimed that he had witnessed the young king's death with his own eyes. Convinced that the day of freedom had dawned, the demos voted to send troops to Boeotia and help Thebes throw off the Macedonian yoke. The Thebans, encouraged by Athenian support, launched their revolt. They deposed their puppet government, assaulted and killed two Macedonians stationed in Thebes, and enclosed the rest of the garrison troops inside a barricade. Word of these moves found its way to Alexander, who, as the Greeks soon learned, was very much alive.

Events then unfolded so quickly that they are largely a blur in our sources. Alexander brought his army south toward Thebes at incredible speed, covering some twenty miles a day over rough terrain. Perhaps because they learned of his approach, or perhaps because Phocion persuaded them to change their minds, the Athenians never delivered the aid they had promised. The Thebans stood alone when Alexander arrived and began a pitched battle outside their walls, finally breaking through their defenses and gaining control of the gates. He wreaked a terrible vengeance on the rebellious city. With a thin legal cover provided by Greeks in his service, Alexander had Thebes razed to the ground—an act of destruction more total than anything his father had done at Olynthus. All adult males were put to the sword, and women and children were sold into slavery. The leading land power in Greece was wiped off the map.

Demosthenes' horror and dread, as he followed these events from Athens, can easily be imagined. He was responsible for committing Athens to the revolt, and he had urged Thebes to launch it; he not only bore some blame for the latter city's destruction, he had also put his own in harm's way. The Athenians, shocked by the fate of

Thebes, sent envoys into Boeotia to appease Alexander. They returned with encouraging news: Alexander would not take vengeance on Athens itself, only on the orators who had abetted the Thebans. On the list of those to be handed over, a list comprising some eight or ten men, was the name of Demosthenes.

At a tense Assembly meeting, the Athenians debated how to respond to this brutal infringement on their freedom of speech. Three detailed reports survive of this critical session, differing in details but concurring in essentials. All agree that the final stage of debate pitted Phocion, the pragmatist and (in this case at least) appeaser of Macedon, against Demosthenes, speaking now not for a policy but for his own life.

Phocion urged the men on the list to surrender to Alexander. He cited mythic heroines who had gone to their deaths to save Athens, implying that such was the noble and right thing to do. He called to the bema his closest friend, Nicocles, and displayed him to the Assembly; then he pointed to the men on Alexander's Wanted list. "These men," he said, "have brought the city to such a pass that, even if someone demanded Nicocles here, I'd tell you to give him up." He implied that Demosthenes and the others had done so much damage that they *deserved* their fate. Finally he accused the group of cowardice for clinging to their lives. He apparently went too far, since we are told by one source that the Assembly shouted him down and heckled him off the bema.[7]

It was up to Demosthenes, who spoke directly after Phocion, to reply to these arguments. His speech has not survived in full, but parts were later quoted by Plutarch.

Demosthenes began with an animal fable, a parable for the bind that Athens found itself in. A flock of sheep, needing protection from wolves, had hired a group of dogs to serve as their guards. Then the wolves approached the sheep and offered them a pact of non-aggression, provided they dismissed the dogs. The sheep complied, but once their defenders were gone, the wolves broke the pact and devoured the sheep at their leisure. The allegory cast the wanted men as the watchdogs of Athens, defending its liberty against an inveterate foe. Alexander, Demosthenes told the Assembly, should be seen not just as a wolf but as a *monolukos,* a lone wolf, the most savage kind.

Demosthenes then turned to a different analogy, drawn from the marketplace. Sellers of grain, he reminded the crowd, will offer a small portion of their stock as a sample; if the buyer tastes it and approves, they will sell the whole lot. "In the same way," Demosthenes said, "if you give in, in our case, you'll be giving up all of *yourselves,* unaware."[8] The parallel was less apt than that of the sheep and wolves, but the point was clear. If the city did not defend itself against this first incursion, it would never be able to do so later, when the demands multiplied. The time to resist, he implied, was now.

Demosthenes won over many in the Assembly that day, but he and the other wanted men were taking no chances. They pooled their funds and hired Demades, a notorious grafter, to speak on their behalf and to offer to go in person to Alexander. Demades' speech gave the Assembly a way out of an agonizing decision. His motion was passed; Demades was sent to Boeotia as head of a delegation to try to win clemency. It must have rankled Demosthenes to rely on a drunken libertine, as much addicted to pleasure as he himself was to work, but the fall of Thebes had left him a hostage to fortune and to Alexander's temper.

Reports differ as to what happened next. One source claims that Demades made a persuasive speech, and Alexander agreed to let Athens punish its own, without intervention. Another says that Alexander became incensed, refused to listen to Demades, and threw the man's rescript across the room in disgust; only after a second speech, this one delivered by Phocion, did the angry young monarch relent. Whatever took place, Athens managed to gain most of what it had sought. Demosthenes' life and the lives of his fellow orators were spared; Alexander insisted on one extradition only, that of a certain Charidemus. That man fled into exile, so all, in the end, were spared the jaws of the lone wolf.

Using both the power of words and the influence that money could buy, Demosthenes had maneuvered out of a very tight spot. But the episode of the Theban revolt had weakened him badly. He had urged his city into *another* fight that endangered its safety and had given false hope to Thebes, in part by his assertion that Alexander was dead. His wings were clipped even shorter than they had been after Chaeronea, and his voice became further muted. Meanwhile Demades, who helped him get out of his jam, and Phocion, who cautioned Athens not to jump in with the Thebans, accrued enormous credit with the Assembly. In the new age that was dawning—the era of Alexander—it would be these men and other accommodationists who would guide Athenian policy choices, not Demosthenes.

When the dust of ruined Thebes had settled, Diondas pressed his indictment of Hyperides for proposing, illegally as he claimed, to have Demosthenes honored with a crown. The charge meant that Demosthenes was also, by implication, in the dock along with Hyperides; the two men had worked so closely together, first on Chaeronea and then on the Theban revolt, as to form a single target. Later, as will be seen, their partnership would come unglued, then glued together again, in sync with enormous changes in world events.

We know little of what Diondas said at the trial brought on by his suit, and we knew nothing of Hyperides' speech of defense,

"Against Diondas," until 2008. In that year a large part of the speech was recovered from the Archimedes palimpsest, a parchment codex erased by a scribe in the thirteenth century and overwritten with a collection of psalms. With the help of ultraviolet and infrared light and X-ray technology, researchers have peered beneath the top layer of ink and extracted the largely erased text beneath. From this invaluable source have come two works of Archimedes, the great mechanical engineer and mathematician, as well as portions of two speeches by Hyperides, one of them "Against Diondas." For some unknown reason the ancient scribe who created the original codex included this purely political tract, along with a second speech prosecuting a civil case, in a volume concerned with physics and higher math.

In the recovered portion of "Against Diondas," Hyperides dealt with the Theban alliance of 338, engineered by Demosthenes, and with the dismal outcome of Chaeronea. As Demosthenes did in his funeral oration, Hyperides attributed that outcome to luck, not to policy failure. "If, jurymen, you were worsted in battle, that's nothing remarkable," he argued. "But you were worsted while choosing the valuable path, believing that you must, by facing dangers, set the Greeks free as you did in the past."[9] The reasons for fighting the war, he insisted — a war he compared to the glorious fight against Persia in the days of Xerxes' invasion — were not rendered any less valid by the defeat of the Greeks. Indeed, a loss in a righteous cause could be seen as a moral victory, as in the case of the three hundred Spartans who died at Thermopylae.

Hyperides asked the jury to think themselves back in time, to just after the seizure of Elateia, when Thebes had had to choose between Athens and Philip. If a speaker *then* had promised to bring Thebes over to the Athenian side, would the jurors not think that this hypothetical person was worthy of the greatest rewards? Yet this was exactly what Demosthenes and Hyperides had achieved. "And consider this too, Athenians: If we had been arrested and tried before Philip, what would be the charge against us? . . . That we dissolved the alliance he had with the Thebans, and made them *your* allies? What punishment would we have gotten from him? Wouldn't we have been executed? I think so."[10] With such shifts of perspective, Hyperides drew the minds of the jury away from the battle itself and back toward the hopeful developments that preceded it.

At one point Hyperides noted the presence of dispossessed Thebans among the spectators attending the trial. Alexander had barred the Greeks from receiving Thebans into their cities, but Athens had defied that order and taken in all who arrived there. These survivors and refugees, "who are at leisure, though I could wish they weren't," had a strong moral interest in the trial's outcome. In an oblique reference to the recent Theban revolt, Hyperides urged the jury not to disillusion these men. "How would they not justly accuse you, if you convict me for the same cause to which you summoned them?"[11] To judge that fighting at Chaeronea was wrong would also mean judging the Theban revolt, encouraged by Athens, wrong, and thus make Athens guilty of leading Thebes to destruction for no good reason.

The twists of logic were sinuous, but not unusually so for Athens in its golden age of oratory. Talented speakers in those days attained leadership because the city they dwelt in was fantastically logophilic; verbal dexterity conferred political power. Trials that played out before huge juries of up to fifteen hundred men, with speeches that occupied hours, caused sensations in Athens, drawing huge crowds with displays of the utmost that the Greek language, and human reason, could do. Demosthenes and Hyperides were to be the last two giants of that golden age, destined to bring down its curtain with their deaths.

Hyperides triumphed in his clash with Diondas, bringing redemption as well to Demosthenes. Diondas failed to carry a fifth of the jurors' votes, which meant that under Athenian law he was fined a thousand drachmas for frivolous prosecution and forbidden to bring further charges. The faction that hated Demosthenes and wanted him punished for Chaeronea, for the destruction of Thebes, and for two decades of waning Athenian power had been dealt an embarrassing blow. But his enemies were not done with him yet.

In the spring of 334 Alexander brought his army across the straits into Asia, fulfilling the plans laid down and begun by his father. The greatest, most consequential military campaign in the history of the world was now under way. Demosthenes did nothing, except, no doubt, pray for its defeat. "Did you give any speech at that time, Demosthenes, or move any decree?" Aeschines later taunted. "Or should I assume that you were afraid?"[12] But Demosthenes was more discouraged than fearful. He had used his rhetorical skills to the full for nearly two decades, yet the city's position had grown steadily worse.

The historical record has little trace of Demosthenes over the next several years. Even when the Spartans launched a war against Macedon, raising a revolt while Alexander was far away, Demosthenes, Plutarch writes, "stirred himself only feebly in support." Other sources claim he did even less than that — nothing at all.[13] The Spartans stood nearly alone against Antipater, head of Alexander's home guard, without Athenian help.

Demosthenes' grand public speeches were mostly behind him, for Athens no longer had big decisions to make. But those made in past years still haunted the city and would not be laid to rest. In 330, as Alexander drove eastward, Aeschines stepped forward once more to pin the blame on Demosthenes for what had gone wrong. He revived his indictment, lodged six years earlier, that the motion of Ctesiphon to award a gold crown to Demosthenes had been illegal.

Though not himself charged with wrongdoing, Demosthenes took up Aeschines' challenge, agreeing to speak in place of Ctesiphon at the trial. The final battle between these two speakers would not be fought by proxy but mano a mano.

CHAPTER NINE

He's a Greek-Speaking Barbarian!

The world had changed rapidly in the years preceding the trial of Ctesiphon, faster perhaps than in any previous era. "What unexpected or unlooked-for thing has not come about in our time?" Aeschines asked the jury in his prosecutorial speech "Against Ctesiphon." "We have not lived a life of human dimensions, but rather we were born to be a source of amazement to those who will come after us."[1] He proceeded to list some of the transformations, including two recent developments involving Alexander. Those events, of which one was still in progress, may explain his decision to push his indictment, filed six years previously, toward a forensic showdown.

Many in Athens had hoped that Alexander would be defeated in Asia, or killed, but in 330 news arrived that he had triumphed at the Battle of Gaugamela. A vast Persian army had been routed, and Darius had fled into the mountains of Media (in modern Iran). "Is it not true," asked Aeschines in amazement, "that the king of the Persians . . . who dared to write in his letters that he was master of all humankind from the rising to the setting sun, is contending now not to be lord of others but to save his own life?"[2] Alexander had begun styling himself king of Asia, and had gained a great deal more power than he had held just a few weeks before.

At more or less the same moment, the Spartans had gone down to defeat after mounting their revolt against Macedon. "The poor men of Lacedaemon," Aeschines noted, referring to Sparta, ". . . who once claimed the right to be leaders of the Greeks, are now about to be sent to Alexander to serve as hostages and make a display of misfortune."[3] Fifty leading Spartans were being deported deep into what is now Iran, to the camp of Alexander, to ensure that their city would not make trouble again. Athens had stood by impassively during this failed uprising, chastened by the lessons of Thebes. In Europe, as in Asia, in the weeks just before the trial, Macedon had attained greater strength than anyone could have foreseen, and the Greeks had lost nearly all hope of liberation.

None of this had been the fault of Demosthenes, but Aeschines could make it appear otherwise. Appending to his list of Greek woes the decline of Athenian power over two decades, Aeschines made the case in "Against Ctesiphon" that the entire series of setbacks should be laid at Demosthenes' feet. "Navy and army and cities have been obliterated by his conduct of politics," he inveighed. He quoted some lines from Hesiod's *Works and Days*, an epic poem his audience knew well: "Often a whole city suffers from just one man, / who sins against god and contrives deeds of wickedness," then added, "If you take away the poet's meter and examine his intentions, I think this passage will seem to you not Hesiod's poem but an oracle directed at Demosthenes' politicking."[4] The second-most revered of Greek bards, yielding only to Homer, was thus brought into court as a prosecution witness.

Aeschines spent only a little of his allotted time on Ctesiphon, the ostensible defendant. His real target was Demosthenes, and he was aware that when he finished his speech, it would be Demosthenes, not Ctesiphon, who would frame the reply; court procedure allowed those on trial to yield their speaking time to supporters. At various points in his speech Aeschines anticipated what his opponent would say or how he would say it. He mocked Demosthenes' habit of "whirling yourself around in a circle upon the bema" (apparently some sort of emphatic gesture), and scoffed at his lush metaphors: "What are these, you fox, words or marvels?" He called the jurors *sideroi*, "men of iron," for having the patience to listen to such excesses.[5] He warned that Demosthenes would use tears and make his voice shrill with emotion to gain his listeners' pity.

Aeschines seemed to have learned in advance the basic lines of Demosthenes' speech of defense, or at least so he claimed. That speech, he predicted, would deal with events of the past in four segments: the war for Amphipolis, the Peace of Philocrates, the war that led to Chaeronea, and the time that followed the battle up to the present. In each case, Aeschines said, Demosthenes would demand to know in what way he did *not* benefit the city. To forestall this approach, Aeschines went through the four time frames himself, showing how his opponent had bungled things or, he alleged, taken bribes to support the wrong cause. He reinvigorated old disputes by bringing new charges, for example by claiming — improbably — that Demosthenes had done even more than Philocrates had to ram the peace treaty with Philip through the Assembly.

Events surrounding Thebes, a city that was now a deserted ruin, loomed large in Aeschines' line of attack. As Hyperides had done in his speech "Against Diondas," Aeschines used the fall of Thebes and the presence of Theban refugees in Athens to stir the jury's emotions. "Look with your imagination at their sufferings," he bid the jurors. "Think that you're seeing the capture of their city, the destruction of their walls, the burning of their homes, their women and children led away into slavery, their aged men and women learning too late what freedom is, wailing, begging you, angry not so much at those taking vengeance on them but at those who are the cause of these things, urging you by no means to give a crown to the scourge of Hellas, but rather to guard against the dark fate and bad luck that accompany the man!"[6] Without specifying the means (beyond a vague allusion to bribery), he implied that Demosthenes had helped ensure the annihilation of Thebes.

In calling Demosthenes the "scourge [*aliterios*] of Hellas," Aeschines was repeating a powerful phrase he had used earlier in his speech. An aliterios was, in its original meaning, a kind of evil divinity bringing destruction. This epithet, followed by the idea that a daimon or dark fate attached to Demosthenes, lent a mythic overlay to the speech's account of events. Demosthenes, we recall, had invoked bad luck, tyche, to explain bad policy outcomes, especially at Chaeronea; Hyperides had agreed with that explanation. Aeschines turned the argument on its head, suggesting that the bad luck had taken on human form. Starting a line of attack that others would later pursue, he cast Demosthenes as a curse destined to bring ruin to every endeavor.

In another visualization exercise, Aeschines bid the jurors imagine themselves in the Theater of Dionysus at the start of the annual tragic performances. This was the time and place at which, in Ctesiphon's motion, Demosthenes would have received his crown—a highly charged occasion when much of Athens, and members of many Greek states, would be present. It was also the time at which, traditionally, a herald honored the city's young men whose fathers had died in battle. Aeschines wrung much pathos from the contrast between the two rituals. He pictured the herald cringing with shame as he announced Demosthenes' crown, "standing beside the man who is the cause of the children's fatherlessness"—the man who, as he claimed, had disgracefully run from the battle he himself had instigated. "I beg you, by Zeus and the gods," Aeschines implored, "not to set up a monument of your own defeat in the orchestra of the theater, not to convict the Athenian demos of madness in the presence of the Greeks."[7]

Picturing the award of the crown in a setting that belied its meaning was one way to sway the jury; character assassination was another. Though he did not use the term "Batalus" in this speech, the nickname he had given such lurid associations, Aeschines did hint vaguely at what he claimed was his opponent's scandalous sex life. He mentioned a certain Aristion, a good-looking boy who had lived for a time in Demosthenes' house, then added, in a classic rhetorical ploy, "Stories vary about what this boy did or had done to him, and it's not at all proper for me to discuss the matter." He used the same ploy a second time, making obscure but salacious suggestions: "The way he [Demosthenes] has used his own body, and his manner of siring children, are such that I decline to say what he's done; for I've seen in the past that those who speak too clearly about the shameful deeds of their neighbors incur ill-will."[8]

With surprising boldness, Aeschines tried at one point in the speech to depict Demosthenes, defender of democracy and free speech, as anti-democratic. He listed five qualities that, in his view, distinguished the "democratic man" from the "oligarchic man," then went on to show that Demosthenes lacked all five. He began with the question of lineage. Those born to citizen parents, whose legal status was secure, had no need for regime change, he reasoned; only those who were less well established caused revolutions. He traced Demosthenes' line through three generations. We cannot assess the accuracy of this genealogy, but it purports to show that Demosthenes "was born to a Scythian mother — he's a Greek-speaking barbarian!"[9] The degree to which this nettled Demosthenes, who saw himself as a champion of Hellenism, is evident in the way he hit back on the parentage question in his own speech.

Other "oligarchic" qualities listed by Aeschines concerned life-style and management of finances. Since debtors too had a motive to seek regime change, misuse of money was anti-democratic. Demosthenes had always been well-off, but Aeschines made the case that he had squandered his family wealth as a youth and gone into politics to repair his fortunes. Then that income too ran through Demosthenes' fingers, leading him to seek new funds — by skimming off payments from Persia. As everyone knew, the Persians had been funneling money to men in Greece who could harm the Macedonian cause, and Demosthenes had been one of their principal agents. In Aeschines' view, this amounted to profiteering by fomenting a war that Athens then lost. "To sum it all up," Aeschines admonished the jury, "he gets his livelihood not from personal earnings, but from the dangers to *you*."[10]

Again and again, using various terms, Aeschines made his opponent out to be a liar. He called him an *alazon,* a boastful quack; a *goes,* dark enchanter; a *ballantotomios,* sneak thief (literally "cut-purse"); and a *sukophantes,* a filer of false prosecutions. He warned the jury about the deceptions they would hear when Demosthenes had his turn. "The man behaves differently from the norm. Other deceivers try to speak vaguely and ambiguously when they tell lies, fearing they'll be caught out. But when Demosthenes deceives, he first swears a lying oath, calling destruction down on himself; next, when speaking of things he knows will never be, he dares to say *when* they will happen, and recites the names of people he has never even seen the faces of . . . mimicking those speaking truth."[11] Use of persuasive specifics made Demosthenes more heinous, Aeschines explained, because "he destroys the signs of good men" — like an expert forger who makes *all* documents seem invalid.

Among the "lies" Aeschines claimed the jury would hear from Demosthenes was one concerning Aeschines' motive for bringing his suit to trial. "He'll say that I wrote the indictment not out of concern for the city, but to catch Alexander's eye," Aeschines predicted.[12] That idea had no doubt already occurred to some jurors, which is why Aeschines raised it. Since Alexander was known to despise Demosthenes, it was plausible (and still is) that Aeschines consulted Macedon before prosecuting his case, or at least hoped to gain that nation's favor afterward.

Aeschines ended by calling on a strange pantheon to witness the justice of his case. "O Earth, and Sun, and Virtue, and Intelligence, and Learning by which we distinguish the good from the shameful — I have come to my city's aid and I have spoken," he incanted.[13] The water trickling through the device that measured his time allotment was nearly gone. Demosthenes was preparing to make his rebuttal.

The speech Demosthenes gave that day is known as "On the Crown" (or *De Corona* in Latin), rather than "For Ctesiphon," the usual format for titles of defense speeches. It might just as well be referred to as "For Demosthenes," since its subject, as its author pointed out in his opening, was "my entire private life and my public political record." In part it is also "Against Aeschines," for in it Demosthenes set out to destroy his chief opponent once and for all. He unleashed his rhetorical weapons in two fusillades, hitting back a good deal harder than he had been hit.

At the center of the speech stood the question of policy toward Philip, still controversial eight years after Chaeronea. Many Athenians must have looked back on that time with regret, thinking that they could have prospered and spared the lives of husbands, sons, and brothers had they joined Philip or simply stayed neutral rather than taking the field. Demosthenes gave no ground on this point. Philip, he argued, had aimed at "tyranny over the Greeks," "rule over the Greeks," and even "the enslavement of all humankind."[14] Athens had been right to oppose him, unlike those who took his side — the Thessalians are singled out — who thereby "share the blame for the bad and shameful outcome" of the present. Indeed, he asserted, Athens had cause to be proud of its anti-Philip record. "Let all the 'crimes' and 'blunders' that have been committed be ascribed to *me,*" Demosthenes urged; "but if there were need for someone to come forward to stop these things, who else ought it to have been except the Athenian demos?"[15]

Having thus laid down an initial defense of the claim, as stated in Ctesiphon's motion, that he had spoken and acted in his city's interest, Demosthenes turned his glare on Aeschines. Despite his contention that he was "not fond of hurling barbs," he fired a salvo of highly original insults, calling Aeschines a *spermologos,* "seed-picker" (like a bird that survives by pillaging farmers' fields), a *peritrimm'agoras,* "marketplace layabout," and an *olethros grammateus,* "pestilent clerk" (deriding one of Aeschines' earlier government posts). Quoting from the last words of "Against Ctesiphon," in which Aeschines had called on Earth, Sun, Virtue, Intelligence and Learning, Demosthenes rejoined: "What part of Virtue belongs to you or your kind, you piece of filth? . . . How is it right for you even to mention Learning?"[16] He linked the grandiose peroration to Aeschines' youthful stint as a tragic performer, implying his foe had been chewing the scenery.

Aeschines had brought the issue of parentage into the trial, and Demosthenes showed that he was more than ready to fight on this turf. Thirteen years earlier, in his speech "On the False Embassy," Demosthenes had referred to Aeschines' father as a teacher named Atrometus, a name that signifies courage. Now he asserted that the man's real name was Tromes, "Trembles," and that he was *enslaved* to a teacher, forced to wear iron shackles and a wooden punishment collar. Then, referring to Aeschines' mother, whom he had earlier called Glaucothea (Gray-eyed Goddess), Demosthenes cranked up the vitriol. Her real name was Empusa, he claimed, connecting her to a shape-shifting, mythical monster, "because she does everything and has everything done to her." He depicted her as a cheap prostitute "who makes use of the shed by the shrine of the hero Calamite for her midday nuptials," that is, for turning tricks.[17]

Whether these charges were true was irrelevant; in fact, Demosthenes' own earlier speech makes clear they likely were not. Belittlement was the objective, and these images of Aeschines' parents, a slave wearing irons and a sexually versatile whore, accomplished his goal well enough. But Demosthenes was just getting started. He asserted that the young Aeschines was his mother's "pretty little plaything," as though he were a homunculus, and a "top-notch C-list actor," someone who always got the smallest parts in a tragic performance. Then he started in on Aeschines' political career, portraying it as a mix of bribe taking, traitorous backroom dealings, and, above all, inaction when Athens most needed action. Aeschines' role in launching the Fourth Sacred War, proudly touted by Aeschines himself in "Against Ctesiphon," was now described — perhaps with some justification, as we saw in Chapter 6 — as a scheme to bring Philip back into central Greece.

As always in debates of this era, the Battle of Chaeronea loomed large at the Ctesiphon trial. Aeschines, in his prosecutorial speech, had harped on the theme of policy failure and on Demosthenes' desertion of his post. Demosthenes did not address the charge of cowardice, but he had plenty to say about whether the battle was wise. As his ally Hyperides had done, and as he had done himself in his funeral speech, Demosthenes made the case that bad luck, a force beyond human control, led to the outcome of Chaeronea. "Don't make it my fault, if it fell to Philip to prevail in the battle," he said, addressing Aeschines directly. "The outcome lay with the god, not with me." He compared himself to a sea captain who had taken every measure to safeguard his ship but still saw the rigging torn by a violent storm. Such a captain would say, as Demosthenes did, "I was not master of fortune, but fortune was master of all."[18]

The strongest defense of Chaeronea came in a section Demosthenes himself considered risky, to judge by the way he begged his listeners not to be shocked. The argument that begins it is indeed shocking: "If everything that was going to happen" – defeat in the battle – "were clear beforehand and everyone knew in advance, and if you, Aeschines, spoke out in advance and protested by screaming and shouting (you who never said a word!), not even in *that* circumstance ought the city to have avoided these things, if it esteemed either its reputation, or our ancestors, or the ages to come."[19] The idea that Athens ought to have marched to certain defeat is implausible but rhetorically brilliant. Athenian losses at Chaeronea had already been compared, as we saw, to the deaths of the Spartan three hundred at Thermopylae, an instance (in the Greek view) of glorious self-sacrifice.

Demosthenes then paid a stirring tribute to his city's historical role in leading the fight for freedom. In the Persian Wars of the previous century, Athenians had defied Xerxes when others had met his demands for submission. They had even stoned to death a certain Cursilus, along with his wife, for proposing, just before the decisive Battle of Salamis, that Athens collaborate with Xerxes and grant him sovereignty. The Athenians had chosen to follow their heroic leader Themistocles instead, "for they did not think life worth living, if they could not live in freedom."[20] The historical parallel implicitly cast Aeschines as Cursilus and Demosthenes as

Themistocles – but, due simply to misfortune, a Themistocles who had lost.

The legacy of the Persian Wars had been glorious for Athens, but Demosthenes argued that the city would lose its glory if the jury now sided with Aeschines. Such a verdict would amount to declaring that Athens was wrong to fight at Chaeronea, thereby robbing the effort of all moral meaning. "But you cannot, you cannot have been wrong, Athenians, to have taken on the danger of fighting for the freedom and safety of all!" Rising to a crescendo, he swore to his sincerity not by the gods but by the Persian War dead: "I swear by those of your ancestors who faced peril at Marathon, and by those who formed their ranks at Plataea, and by those in the sea fights at Salamis and Artemisium, and many others laid in public tombs." In the midst of this climax, he turned to address Aeschines: "They were good men, all of whom the city buried in the same manner, deeming them worthy of the same honor, Aeschines – not the successful or the victorious alone. And justly so – for all had done the work that falls to good men, though their luck was that which the god assigned to each one."[21]

This passage rises to such lofty levels that several centuries later a critic of style, Dionysius of Halicarnassus, quoted it as an example of oratorical brilliance. Dionysius ended his quote, sensibly, at the point reached here. But Demosthenes used the elevation he had gained to resume hurling insults at Aeschines, calling him a *grammatokuphon*, a "hunchback clerk" (one stooped over from scrutinizing papers), and, once again, a *tritagonistes*, an actor who gets only minor roles. After soaring along in the heights, Demosthenes descended to the depths with astonishing speed. In fact a cynic might say that he had soared to those heights only to add momentum to the dive bomb. "The abrupt shift from grandeur to derision . . . is an attempt to crush Aeschines when Demosthenes is most imposing," commented the classicist Harvey Yunis in a recent edition of "On the Crown." As with all Athenian orators of this era, the role of high-minded statesman combines uneasily, from our point of view, with that of bare-knuckled brawler.[22]

Demosthenes returned to brawling as he neared the end of his speech, in a passage preceded by another plea for indulgence. "By Zeus, let no one think poorly of me for any coldness," he begged, using a term that connotes a repellent lack of taste. He went on to impugn Aeschines for his impoverished upbringing, a strategy that carried risks — "I don't think anyone who insults poverty is a sensible person" — but he felt, he claimed, that he had no choice. "I am forced to enter into these discussions by this man's slanderous, lying accusations." Aeschines had been the first to take off the gloves.[23]

Contrasting his own, wealthy childhood with that of Aeschines, Demosthenes claimed for himself the background and education of an upstanding citizen. Aeschines by contrast had drifted from one ignoble trade to another, pursuing wealth with such urgency that he had lost his moral compass. He had started out helping his father in the schoolroom, preparing ink and sweeping the floor, "the station of a servant, not a free youth." Then he had apprenticed himself to his mother, imagined here not as a prostitute but as leader of an ecstatic religious cult. He had assisted in her weird rites, putting fawn skins on her followers and helping them wash with a scrub made of clay and oat bran. Aeschines' next jobs were the two professions Demosthenes constantly mocked, a low-level government clerkship and an amateur turn on the tragic stage. "You played the bit parts," Demosthenes sneered of the latter career, "while collecting figs, grapes, and olives like a fruit seller poaching on other people's fields."[24] The triple insult showed Aeschines performing so badly as to have fruit thrown at him, being so poor that he had to gather the fruit, and keeping or selling fruit that was not his own, like a common thief.

To say, in effect, "he started it" to excuse these low blows was disingenuous on Demosthenes' part. In fact *he* had started it sixteen years earlier when he indicted Aeschines on the charge of false dealing in his embassy to Philip. Aeschines had delivered some low blows in the trial that resulted, calling Demosthenes Batalus and giving that name unsavory sexual meaning. But Demosthenes aimed even lower blows here. His caricature of Aeschines in "On the Crown" as the son of a slave and a whore who had struggled as a menial scribe and a talentless actor before finding his true calling in selling out Athens for bribes reduced his opponent to minuscule, mean proportions. At the same time he enlarged himself by placing the Battle of Chaeronea, his greatest achievement, in a long line of heroic Athenian efforts on behalf of freedom.

Demosthenes ended "On the Crown" with his sole reference to current events, the triumph of Alexander in Asia and the continuing powerlessness of Athens. He indicated that in his mind the fight against Macedon was not over, though he did not dare say so openly. Rather, he alluded vaguely to the "impious people" in Athens who looked "outside" (to Macedon or to Asia) and rejoiced when "someone else" (Alexander) enjoyed good fortune at the expense of the Greeks. "All you gods," he implored, addressing the heavens, "put better mind and better thoughts in these people, but if they cannot be cured, destroy and demolish them utterly, as a group, on land and on sea. And to us who remain, grant release from our looming fears as soon as you can, and secure salvation."[25]

This was a combative note on which to end the hours-long speech: a prayer that the pro-Macedonian faction at Athens be annihilated. Demosthenes wanted the city to know that in his eyes at least, the verdict of Chaeronea was not final. The bad luck that had crushed the Greek coalition might turn, and the chance might come to fight for freedom again.

The jurors' ballots were cast in the urns and counted. Demosthenes won his case — officially, Ctesiphon's case — by a wide margin; Aeschines failed to obtain one-fifth of the votes. By Athenian law, he was liable for a large fine, but the greater penalty he incurred was the harm to his reputation. Aeschines soon left Athens, spending the rest of his days in exile, perhaps on the island of Rhodes.

Though he had made a poor showing in arms at Chaeronea, Demosthenes had gained a huge win on his own field of combat, the battleground of words and rhetorical weapons. He had driven his principal foe from that field forever. More important, he had proven a crucial political point through the votes of the huge jury panel. Athenians still stood behind him; they had not rejected his policies or come to despise their earlier choices. Macedon might thus be resisted, if only the gods, or Fortune, tyche, would smile on Athens at last.

CHAPTER TEN

Will You Dare Speak
to Me of Friendship?

Virtually nothing is known of Demosthenes in the six years following "On the Crown," from 330 to 324. No doubt he continued to speak from the bema, but no further political speeches have been preserved. In any case Assembly sessions must have been quieter in the 320s than in previous decades. Athens had few pressing foreign policy choices; Macedon held the reins, while the League of Corinth settled disputes and saw to it that peace between states was maintained. Word trickled back from Asia from time to time, from farther and farther east, describing the astonishing progress of Alexander as he made his way through what is today Afghanistan, Uzbekistan, Tajikistan, and Pakistan. Some of the riches his troops had seized were trickling back as well, helping to make the Pax Macedonica, as some have called it, a prosperous time for Athens and much of the Greek world.

The influx of wealth offered new opportunities, and new temptations, to the Athenians. Phocion, who prided himself on a simple, abstemious lifestyle, watched with dismay as his son took to posh pursuits like the *apobates,* an athletic event that involved jumping on and off a racing chariot. When Phocion went to the young man's house for a victory party, he was met at the door by a slave who was washing guests' feet with wine. This was the last straw for Phocion. He had his son packed off to Sparta, whose citizens still eschewed gold and silver and kept to a "Dorian" regimen of plain food, simple clothing, and vigorous exercise.

Hyperides too, after surviving the legal attacks of Diondas, was enjoying the new prosperity, indulging his taste for rare fish and beautiful women. He reportedly kept three courtesans in his employ, one for each of his three Attic houses. His most famous liaison was with the sought-after Phryne, a Boeotian woman whose body served as the model for two separate masterworks of Greek art: Praxiteles' sculpture of Aphrodite, the Greek world's first full-size female nude, and Apelles' painting of Aphrodite rising from the sea. A kept woman of Phryne's caliber was an expensive proposition, but Hyperides evidently possessed the means.

Far to the east of Athens, in the sumptuous city of Babylon, another playboy was indulging his taste for expensive fish and Greek courtesans, but doing so with funds that were not his own. A Macedonian by the name of Harpalus, a boyhood friend of Alexander's, had been put in charge of the city and of a hoard of riches plundered from the defeated Persians. In 327, as Alexander led his army across the Hindu Kush mountains and into the region the Greeks knew as India, Harpalus raided Babylon's treasury and spent recklessly on his own pleasures. He had a dazzling courtesan, Pythonice, brought over from Athens, and lavished gifts on her; when she died soon afterward (presumably from disease), he had two costly monuments built, one in Babylon and a second in Athens. Then he sent for another Athenian woman, Glycera, and lavished gifts on *her.*

Before long Harpalus had incurred massive debts, too great for Alexander to forgive should he return from the East. Harpalus must have hoped that that return would never happen, but as a safeguard he built up credit in Athens by donating money for public events. The grateful Athenians granted him citizenship.

By a strange chain of events, the troubles of this free-spending, high-living man were to land squarely on the Athenian docket and cause new headaches for Demosthenes. After six years of relative calm, the waters of public life were being stirred up again, and Demosthenes had to work harder than ever to steer his way out of the riptides.

Part of the new turbulence came from Alexander's decision to rearrange the Greek world with a wave of his mighty hand. It was learned in the spring of 324 that the king, making his way westward from what is now Pakistan, was going to require all the Greek states to take back the citizens they had sent into exile and restore their legal rights. A decree to be read out at that summer's Olympic Games threatened action by Antipater, head of the Macedonian home guard, against any state that did not comply. Alexander was determined to neutralize the threat these exiles might pose if some emerging Greek leader formed them into an army, for by now their numbers were huge. He was unconcerned that his blanket pronouncement sidestepped the League of Corinth, the synod at which the Greek states were supposed to make such decisions or at least give approval to those made by Macedon.

All the Greek states had reason to dread this Exiles Decree, but to Athens it posed a particular threat. Years earlier, Athens had seized the island of Samos, in the eastern Aegean, and booted out its inhabitants, then awarded their lands to needy Athenians; Samos became, in effect, an overseas province of Athens. The Exiles Decree would force the reversal of this land grab and the restoration of Samians to their homeland. Dismay at the prospect ran as high in the Assembly as it had once run in the case of Amphipolis, another distant region that the Athenians, with their imperial mindset, regarded as their own but had lost. Feelings about Macedon may have been mixed, but on the Samos question Athens had a single, strong resolve.

Alexander crafted the Exiles Decree in late winter 324, by which time he had reached Susa in present-day Iran. Watching his westward progress, Harpalus, the rogue treasurer who had been recklessly squandering funds, knew he would not survive if Alexander reached him in Babylon. He formed a convoy of six thousand mercenaries and mules to haul chests of coin, then left his post and headed for the Aegean. When the seas had grown calm enough (perhaps in mid-March), he filled thirty ships with his troops and treasure and set sail for Athens. He intended to give the city he had befriended, the least damaged of the major powers of Greece, the chance to revolt against Alexander, using Alexander's own money and manpower to do so.

Athens was already fretting over the terms of the Exiles Decree, brought to its shores by an envoy named Nicanor, when the Harpalus flotilla drew up outside the harbor of Piraeus, awaiting permission to enter. The city now had to deal with two crises that impinged on one another. Perhaps Alexander could be persuaded to grant an exception to the decree, allowing Athens to keep control of Samos; if so, then it might make sense to turn Harpalus away, rather than abet his embezzlement. Alternatively, if Samos were forever lost, or if for other reasons the time seemed ripe for revolt, then Harpalus and his troops could be of great use. Admitting them would bring Athens a windfall, including pots of money with which to hire more troops.

Intertwined with these questions, and complicating both, was a possible third dilemma, though we know next to nothing about it. It seems that at some point in 324 Alexander made known he expected the Greeks to worship him as a god – or perhaps his allies in Greece made the proposal on his behalf. He may have felt that he needed superhuman authority to impose such a sweeping measure as the Exiles Decree. However the idea of worship took shape, it caused yet more angst in the Assembly at Athens, once again pitting appeasers against resisters. Deifying a living mortal defied all religious norms in the eyes of most Greeks, but doing so in this case might mean that Athens could hold on to Samos.

In the days of Philip and during the revolt of Thebes, Demosthenes had led the resisters, but since then he had gradually moved toward the attitude of the appeasers. He had reached the age of sixty and lived fourteen years under Macedon's sway, so perhaps he had mellowed with age; or he may simply have adapted to circumstances. Or perhaps, as his enemies thought, he had been bribed to go along with the new superpower. For whatever reason, when Harpalus anchored offshore and asked for admission, Demosthenes spoke in favor of keeping the harbor closed. His position divided him from Hyperides, his old ally, for Hyperides was still a staunch resister and saw the purloined money as fuel for revolt. But the Assembly vote went Demosthenes' way, and the harbor stayed closed.

The friendship between Hyperides and Demosthenes had always been based on convenience rather than mutual trust. It was said that one day, when Hyperides claimed to be ill, Demosthenes went to his home and found a list there containing his own misdeeds. The idea that his friend had been tabulating his crimes seemed outrageous, but Hyperides coolly explained his logic. "If we remain friends, this list can never hurt you," he said, "but if we fall out, it ensures that you'll never hurt *me*." The story is likely apocryphal, but it gives a credible picture of an alliance that changed with the shifting winds. The Harpalus debate dealt a blow to that bond; more blows were to follow.

Though rejected on his first try, Harpalus, officially an Athenian citizen, did not give up on his quest for refuge. He made a brief stop in the Peloponnese to release his troops, then returned to Athens and once again asked for admission. Officers sent by Alexander, by Antipater in Macedon, and even by Alexander's mother were by now on his trail. He still had a great deal of money with him, and according to later reports, he spread it around to anyone who could help him. But charges of bribery and graft were so rife in this era, and so hard to prove, that we cannot know which were factual and which political mudslinging. The Athenians could not know either, though they made their assumptions.

Turning away a suppliant, especially a citizen, was against Athenian principles, but welcoming him and accepting his ill-gotten wealth risked drawing an attack by Antipater. There was a third option: detaining Harpalus and holding his money in trust, in hopes of gaining leverage for the coming discussions concerning Samos. At an urgent Assembly meeting, Demosthenes, who had earlier argued for closing the harbor, now advocated this third course – a change of stance that would later appear suspicious. The Assembly again voted to do as Demosthenes had advised; Harpalus was put under arrest and his wealth confiscated. He reported that his stolen money came to seven hundred talents, enough for a sizable army. The chests of coin were removed from his ships, with Demosthenes helping to supervise, and brought to the Acropolis for safekeeping.

With the purloined funds in escrow and Harpalus in prison, Demosthenes embarked on another official duty. He had been elected *architheoros* for that year, head of the Athenian contingent attending the Olympic festival. It was a prestigious job and especially sensitive on this occasion, since Nicanor, Alexander's envoy, would be at the games to announce the Exiles Decree. If Athens had any hope of mitigating the edict, it lay with Nicanor. Demosthenes' post was thus part ceremonial, part diplomatic; he was charged with making the case for a stay of the Exiles Decree in the case of Samos. Other Greek states were also sending envoys to meet with Nicanor, since the return of throngs of exiles, many embittered against those in power, spelled trouble nearly everywhere in Greece.

Events are blurred in the historical record from this point forward, and we have no direct testimony from Demosthenes. Whatever parley he held with Nicanor, if any, came to nothing; the Exiles Decree was read out to the Greeks as planned, and thousands of exiles in attendance at the Olympic games roared their approval. Meanwhile, back in Athens, Harpalus escaped from prison and slipped away from the city. Bribery may have been at work, but it is also possible that his escape was abetted by government agents; his presence in Athens was irksome to Macedon, and Athenians still had hopes of winning some kind of exemption from Alexander. They voted at about this time to send envoys to Asia to plead for a stay.

Apparently the Assembly also approved the granting of divine honors to Alexander, an obvious sop to the king's colossal ego. Demades, long a pro-Macedonian voice in the Assembly, supported the motion with the witty remark that Athens should not lose the earth — that is, Samos — through worrying about the heavens. Demosthenes, for his part, made a comment that showed his resigned acceptance of an unpalatable, though largely symbolic, measure. "So he's a son of Zeus, and of Poseidon too, if that's what he wants," he reportedly told the Assembly.[1]

By now it was August, and Demosthenes had returned from Olympia, resuming his role as a member of the board in charge of the Harpalus money. When those funds were counted, the total came to only half of what had been reported earlier. The shortfall of 350 talents sent the city into a panic. The original 700 had been stolen from Alexander, and if half had been lost, then Athens would have to repay it or else, more than likely, face an attack. Charges and countercharges flew through the city, as everyone pointed a finger at someone else. Many fingers pointed at Demosthenes, who had been among those in charge of the money when it was first brought onshore.

Attempting to calm the situation and exculpate himself, Demosthenes proposed that the Areopagus, the high court of Athens, investigate and decide whom to charge for the crime. If he himself were found guilty, he said, he would voluntarily submit to the death penalty.

In the past, Demosthenes had counted on the Areopagus for support and had even used that body as a weapon against his enemies. But he seems to have lost his credit or strained his relations with his former allies. The council that he helped empower to level charges took six months to deliberate, then charged *him* with the crime, along with at least eight other prominent figures. The indictments specified, on no known grounds, the amount that each of these men had allegedly taken; a vast sum of twenty talents was charged to Demosthenes.

After three decades in public life and countless prosecutions, having survived the shame of Chaeronea and the vitriol of his foes, having triumphed over Aeschines in the Ctesiphon trial, Demosthenes prepared once again to defend himself before the Athenian demos. Among the accusers he would face this time was a former friend and, as he knew, a formidable speaker, Hyperides. Also enlisted to aid the prosecution was a speechwriter named Dinarchus, a relative newcomer to politics. Though only in his mid-thirties, Dinarchus was to play a central role in the Harpalus trials, composing speeches against at least three of the defendants, including a scorching barn burner aimed straight at Demosthenes.

What could have occupied the Areopagus during its half-year investigation? The council had no evidence to examine or witnesses to interrogate (none were produced at the trials that resulted). What had become of the missing money — if it had ever been there to begin with — was shrouded in obscurity then and still is. Significantly, the charges came down at about the time the Athenian envoys returned from Asia, reporting that their efforts with Alexander had been fruitless. With Athens again feeling ill-used, perhaps the court felt free to offer up Demosthenes, and others who had had recent dealings with Macedon, to the people's anger.

The frustrations of the present revived mistrusts of the past. Even though he had been exonerated in the Ctesiphon trial for the disasters at Chaeronea and Thebes, Demosthenes' role in the two episodes appeared in a different light once he was under indictment for graft. If he had taken money from Harpalus, as was alleged, it appeared more likely he had acted badly in other cases. Perhaps, it might seem, he had been working against the city's interests as a Macedonian agent as far back as the Peace of Philocrates, now more than twenty years in the past. Everything in Demosthenes' long career was fair game for his present prosecutors; the judicial system had no statutes of limitations, rules of evidence, or guardrails defining what could be said during trials.

Demosthenes hurt his own cause with a troubling, and to this day confusing, misstep. He apparently made some kind of admission, perhaps to his friends, that he had in fact taken the money but then had given it to the Theoric Fund, the state financial reserve. In other words, he had done the wrong thing for the right reason. In public, though, he denied all wrongdoing and turned his rhetorical fire against the Areopagus. He issued a motion demanding that the council reveal its evidence, and claimed that his indictment was a political act; "oligarchs" on the board were attacking him in order to please Alexander. The fact that he gave different accounts for his actions suggests he had something to hide, but we cannot say what. A generous theory holds that he was part of a covert operation that required funds but could not be revealed for security reasons. (I shall return to this in Chapter 11.)

As the headliner among the accused men, Demosthenes was the first to be tried, before a massive jury of fifteen hundred. A battery of ten orators was chosen to prosecute him, each one speaking in turn before the defense was given its say. Some of these ten, including Hyperides, composed their own speeches, while others delivered words written for them. Dinarchus's speech "Against Demosthenes," which survives nearly intact, was delivered second in the lineup by a speaker whose name is not known. The speech is a fireworks display of vitriol, condemnation, and blame.

In previous high-profile trials, such as the battles between Demosthenes and Aeschines, speakers had shown themselves adept at calling each other names, often inventing creative epithets. Dinarchus, in "Against Demosthenes," took a stab at the insult game but with less ingenuity than his predecessors. He borrowed jabs from earlier speeches: *kataptuston*, a poetic word for someone worthy to be spat upon, memorably used by Demosthenes of Aeschines in "On the Crown"; also "Scythian," "charlatan," and, on two occasions, *therion*, "beastie" or "creature," barbs flung earlier by Aeschines at Demosthenes. The young speechwriter seems to have been learning from his elders. One of his own innovations, however, was having the prosecutor throw a staged fit while spewing insults, becoming tongue-tied with rage. He augmented his invective with an interjection, *exagomai* – "I'm carried away" – as a cue to the speaker to seem to be losing control.

The legal argument of Dinarchus's speech was so thin as to be nonexistent. Without any witnesses or evidence to present, he invoked the authority of the Areopagus, insisting that since that board had indicted Demosthenes, he *must* be guilty. "The board has found against Demosthenes. Why is there need of more words?" his speech demands. He compared the Areopagus with the version of that body depicted in Aeschylus's tragic trilogy *The Oresteia*, as though the present council had been convened by the gods themselves. "What will you do?" his speaker asked of the jury, in outrage at the thought they might defy the gods. "You, who claim to be the most pious of all people! Will you render the judgment of the council invalid, and follow the pattern of wickedness set by Demosthenes? No, Athenians – not if you have any sense!"[2]

Though the charges against those accused concerned the previous year, their entire records were being judged, and the very long record of Demosthenes offered numerous targets. Dinarchus went back a quarter-century in his review to an episode earlier targeted by Aeschines. In 348 a man named Nicodemus had accused Demosthenes of deserting a military campaign in Euboea, when in fact he had left the campaign legitimately to conduct official duties at home. Before the trial could take place, Nicodemus was found killed and mutilated, his eyes gouged out and his tongue cut off. The murder was charged to a madman named Aristarchus, but since Demosthenes benefited by it, some said that he had arranged it. In Dinarchus's retelling, the murderer Aristarchus becomes the victim, pushed by the "evil genius" Demosthenes into a violent crime.[3] "You all know the story," Dinarchus's speaker told the jury, a sure sign that after twenty-five years, very few people did.

Dinarchus hit hardest when discussing the Theban revolt of 335, using the time-honored strategy of turning pity for Thebes into anger against Demosthenes. It was rumored that Demosthenes had been given money by Persia to support the revolt (the fantastic sum of three hundred talents was mentioned), but that he had declined to use those funds at a critical moment. A corps of Arcadian troops had been willing to aid the Thebans but instead had stopped midway in the march toward Thebes, demanding a payment of ten talents before proceeding. Demosthenes, according to the charge revived by Dinarchus, had refused to pay, and the troops had stayed put. "On account of this traitor," Dinarchus's speech inveighs, "the wives and children of the Thebans have been divided among the tents of the barbarians [the Macedonians], a city of neighbors and allies has been wrenched up from the middle of Greece, and the site once held by the Thebans is being plowed and sown. . . . Plowed, I tell you, and sown!"[4] The story links the tragic fate of Thebes to Demosthenes' greed, a highly effective ploy in a trial about graft.

Dinarchus asked the jurors to impose the death penalty, and to ease their discomfort at doing so he cited recent precedents. "You condemned Themistius of Aphidna to death," he has his speaker say, addressing the jury as though it were the entire citizen body, "because of an act of violence against the Rhodian lyre player at Eleusis; you condemned Euthymachus to death because he put the little girl from Olynthus into a brothel."[5] These executions for petty crimes, otherwise unknown to history, attest to the harshness of the Athenian courts, in which jurors had often been stirred to a frenzy of outrage before they cast their secret votes. The playwright

Aristophanes, a century before this trial, had lampooned the system's severity by imagining a panel of jurors as a swarm of wasps.

After nearly an hour spent lobbing such bombs, Dinarchus's speaker "handed over the water" to the next prosecutor, the equivalent of yielding time in a modern legislative debate (time was measured by a water clock called a clepsydra). The eight speeches that followed must have been quite a bit shorter since the entire trial, including equal time for the defendant, had to conclude within a single day. At some point in the sequence, perhaps in final position for greatest effect, Hyperides stepped forward, no doubt to enormous anticipation. Not only was this man renowned as an orator, he had also, as everyone knew, been Demosthenes' friend and political ally through much of their lives.

The speech Hyperides gave on this occasion, also known as "Against Demosthenes," was lost until the nineteenth century, when large stretches were found on a tattered papyrus. Where the speech "Against Diondas," recovered from the Archimedes Palimpsest, gives insight into the partnership of Hyperides and Demosthenes in the 330s, this other lucky find illuminates its breakdown a decade later.

Hyperides used that breakdown as part of his prosecutorial strategy, making clear to the jury that he felt betrayed by his friend. "Will you dare speak to me of friendship?" he asked Demosthenes in the course of the speech. "You yourself destroyed that friendship when you took gold to oppose your country's interests. . . . You brought shame on those who took part in your policies in former years."[6] Hyperides was one of those partisans, so his stress on shame had a distinctly personal slant.

In contrast to Dinarchus, Hyperides spent little time on Demosthenes' past record—sensibly, since he had shared it. He alluded only briefly (at least in the extant portion) to the revolt of Thebes. His emphasis was rather on the present and even on the future that might have been. "When we could have had the greatest prestige among the demos," he argued, again implying that his own reputation was linked to that of his colleague, "and the rest of our lives could have been accompanied by a worthy fame, you overturned all that."[7] He spoke with a sorrow that may well have been genuine.

Like Dinarchus, Hyperides leaned heavily on the authority of the Areopagus, and made the case that were Demosthenes to be acquitted, subsequent juries would have to acquit the other defendants as well. "You are judging not just about one crime, but about them all," he told the jurors.[8] This *should* have been true, since all the accused had exactly the same factor weighing against them: a baseless indictment. Yet as the verdicts were handed down, one by one, they differed from defendant to defendant. Those tried later fared better than those whose trials had come early, as the people's anger gradually dissipated.

Demosthenes, who had been tried first and who faced the most anger, drew a guilty verdict. But the jurors did not condemn him to death, as Dinarchus had urged. In fact, the fine they imposed, fifty talents, seems to have been discounted in his favor, since the law required such fines to be ten times the amount of the bribe (that is, two hundred talents in Demosthenes' case). Even so, it was more than Demosthenes could, or was willing to, pay.

Athenian law specified a date by which Demosthenes had to come up with the funds; if he failed, his fine would be doubled, his property would be sold at auction to offset his debt, and he himself would be jailed. In the interim, he was stripped of his citizen rights, a terrible fate for a man who had spent his entire career on the public stage. Unable to speak in the Assembly, barred from all legal proceedings, and facing imprisonment, Demosthenes chose to flee the city. He went into exile in Troezen, directly across the Saronic Gulf from Piraeus.

Demosthenes had preserved his life and his freedom while losing his home, his country, and his citizenship. He was effectively cast out of the demos, the body that had for the past thirty years been his constant milieu. Yet even so, he had not given up on politics. Since he could not make speeches in the Assembly, he set to composing letters to be read aloud there, several of which, remarkably, have survived.

CHAPTER ELEVEN

Hide Your Faces for Shame!

The Assembly at Athens often heard letters read aloud from diplomats, agents abroad, and foreign leaders. Among those missives was the letter from Philip to the people of Athens discussed in Chapter 6, dating perhaps to 340. This was one of several letters by which Philip addressed the Assembly, to judge by references to their contents made by Demosthenes and others. Such letters were stored in state archives, along with the many decrees that had come before the Assembly during its meetings.

Only a few surviving public letters seem to date to the fourth century BCE, and those that do are not universally accepted as genuine. Some, at least, are clearly not what they purport to be. Ancient rhetoricians are known to have written letters pseudonymously, a means to sharpen argument skills by imitating a famous person addressing a critical issue. I have treated the letter of Philip as genuine, but some scholars have challenged its attribution or left the question of authorship unresolved. Indeed, that question can never be fully resolved, for the genuineness of an ancient letter can never be proven; judgments must rest on likelihood, based on style and usage, historical content, and consistency with the author's other writings (a metric that cannot be applied in the case of Philip).

Six public letters survive among the works of Demosthenes, all purporting to date from the time of his exile from Athens (323–322). One of the six seems to be the work of an impersonator; a second is too short for meaningful analysis. The other four were examined in depth in *The Letters of Demosthenes* (1968) by the classicist Jonathan Goldstein, who declared that three were almost certainly genuine, while the fourth was likely to be so. Goldstein's book was hailed as conclusive by most of the scholars who reviewed it, but one reviewer demurred on the grounds that a brilliant forger could have passed all the tests that Goldstein used to prove authenticity. In the reviewer's opinion, the authorship question remained open.

I have elected to follow Goldstein's findings, and my own judgment, by treating three of these six letters as the authentic work of Demosthenes. I believe that the documents are not only genuine but hugely important; they reveal Demosthenes' thoughts as he met his gravest crisis and as his city went through yet another upheaval, the last of his life.

From his place of exile in Troezen, Demosthenes got word of the ongoing Harpalus trials, including the later acquittals. He sensed that the mood in Athens was changing and, as often happened, regret was setting in after the public's anger was sated. He sent a series of letters, the first of which does not survive but is known by report, asking the Assembly to reconsider his verdict or at least give him leave to raise money to pay his fine. Evidently he wanted his citizen rights restored so he could return to the city with dignity; once there, he could try to raise the fifty talents before the amount was automatically doubled.

Demosthenes found especially galling the acquittal of Aristogiton, whom many considered a rogue and who had already done a stint in prison for debt. "You are too unfeeling," Demosthenes wrote in a second letter, speaking to the entire demos via the Assembly, "and you don't feel shame before others or on your own behalf, since you let Aristogiton go for the same offenses for which you banished Demosthenes." He complained that others of the accused had been granted the right, denied to him, to stay in the city and raise the amount of their fines by soliciting loans from friends. He himself was owed a considerable sum by someone to whom he had made such a loan; he planned to get some of it back and raise other funds too, "if you will humanely, and not spitefully, grant me safe leave to tend to these things," that is, by restoring his rights.[1]

The letter in which Demosthenes made this plea, later titled "Concerning Lycurgus's Sons," was not ostensibly concerned with the Harpalus case. His goal in writing it, it seems, was to gain the Assembly's support for the sons of a former ally, Lycurgus, who had been brought to trial by one of their political enemies, also a foe of his own. He began the letter by claiming that he was writing to promote not his own cause but that of Lycurgus's sons. Yet at about the three-quarters point, he diverged from his theme to address his own situation. His ardent tone in the last segment suggests that this was his primary goal all along, but since in his earlier letter he'd focused on his own needs, he judiciously foregrounded others' needs in this one.

He began this final section by scolding the Athenians for their treatment of him and predicting that they would soon regret it. "At some point, you will say that I've been terribly treated, I know this well; but at that point it will do neither you nor me any good," he wrote, implying that he would be dead by that time, a victim of the city's injustice. "And I swear you won't be able to show that I took anything from Harpalus," the letter continues, becoming more strident. "That was not proved against me, and I didn't take it. If you look for justification to the august authority of the council [the Areopagus]," Demosthenes told the Assembly, aware that he was growing heated, "then hide your faces for shame when you think of the verdict passed on Aristogiton!"[2] His point was the same one urged by his prosecutors, that there should be a single verdict for all the defendants; since there had now been one acquittal, all the defendants should likewise be acquitted.

"Don't suppose that I'm speaking these words in anger, for I could never feel that way toward you," the letter continues, cooling in tone as it reaches its conclusion. "Rather, it brings a certain relief to those who are wronged to give voice to what they suffer, just as it helps those in pain to groan aloud."[3] Demosthenes had the difficult task of voicing outrage at his conviction without showing disrespect to the men who had convicted him. His rhetorical skills are clearly under strain. He was aware that petulance would not help his cause, but he could not hold back; the acquittal of Aristogiton had been too much to bear. A man who had done almost nothing to help his city preferred over one who had given it half of his life!

Demosthenes had reason to feel persecuted. Not only were some of the Harpalus defendants being let off, the ones who had been convicted soon saw their sentences mitigated—all but Demosthenes. Even Demades, who admitted his guilt before fleeing the city, was received back after a cooling-off period and, seemingly, forgiven. Demosthenes felt he had been singled out for harsh treatment, and he doubtless understood why. His recent positions regarding the deification of Alexander and the arrest of Harpalus, and his earlier lack of support for the Spartan revolt, had appalled the resistance camp, and before that he had made enemies of the appeasers as well. By adapting to changing circumstances he had estranged those who held fixed positions, either for or against Macedonian rule. Few on either side felt they could trust him, thus few wanted him back in their midst.

The resistance faction, led by Hyperides, was in the ascendant during this time, as Demosthenes surely knew. The Greeks had become aware of fractures within the Macedonian power structure that might provide them with opportunities. Alexander had summoned Antipater, the senior general on the home front, to Babylon, and Antipater had refused to go; it seemed that trouble was brewing between the European and Asian high commands. Seeing how the tide was running, Athens had held on to the Harpalus money, on the pretext that it could be returned only to Alexander himself. Even if half of it had gone missing, it still made a sizable war chest, should Athens need such a thing.

Money had become more potent than ever in the previous months, for the Aegean was filling up with unemployed soldiers for hire. Alexander had forced the governors of his empire to release their Greek mercenaries, to be resettled in accordance with the Exiles Decree. Many of these troops had landed in Taenaron, a virtual no-man's-land in the south of the Peloponnese. The Athenian Boule had taken note of this pool of soldiers and had secretly given funds to Leosthenes, a talented general and a foe of Macedon, to organize and equip an army. Hyperides, who was known to be fond of gambling, was carefully moving Athens closer to taking a very big gamble, a war with Antipater. To conduct such a war, he must have figured, the city would be better off without Demosthenes, a man whom many considered a bad-luck charm.

Whether or not he knew of these secret moves, or even helped advance them, Demosthenes felt he could not stay in Troezen. His criminal conviction had labeled him an ally of the renegade Harpalus and an embezzler of Macedonian wealth; if Alexander demanded his extradition, as had happened before, he could not count on his new hosts to defend him. At some point after dispatching his letter "Concerning Lycurgus's Sons," he relocated to Calauria, an island off the coast of Troezen. The god Poseidon supposedly guarded this island as his special preserve, and a temple located there was thought to protect all suppliants. Even so, Demosthenes did not feel safe. "A man in danger," he wrote in a letter composed on the island, "has only a frail and uncertain security, when outsiders are able to do as they please."[4] By "outsiders" he doubtless meant the Macedonians, by the "man in danger," himself.

This letter, sent from Calauria, later titled "Concerning His Own Return," addresses a single theme, unlike the composite "Concerning Lycurgus's Sons." Demosthenes framed the entire letter as an extended plea to the people of Athens not just for his citizen rights but for total exoneration (as some other defendants had received). The letter oscillates wildly in tone and strategy, sounding at times pathetic and helpless, at other times grandiose, at still other times outraged. In his last great apologia pro vita sua — capping the series that includes "On the Crown" and several defense speeches not preserved in his corpus — he marshaled every argument he could find, regardless of whether some were out of step, logically or rhetorically, with others.

At the opening of the letter, Demosthenes congratulated the Assembly on the recent pardons it had issued, seeing these as signs that an anti-democratic conspiracy had been unveiled. "You have done the right thing, after recognizing that some in the council" — meaning the Areopagus — "were contriving to get lordly power for themselves," he wrote, in language meant to suggest an oligarchic plot. Now that the council's motives were plain to see, "I think that I, if you're willing, should get the same redemption as those who got same accusations, and not be the only one deprived, on a false charge, of homeland and property and the company of my dear ones."[5] That typically laden sentence wraps a demand for justice inside an appeal to pity, and sweetens it all with humility — "if you're willing" (as though the Assembly did anything *un*willingly).

Since an anti-Alexander mood was on the rise in Athens, Demosthenes made vague, defensive allusions to the city's recent accommodations. He admitted to "mistakes" on his own part, without naming them, but blamed the current, compromised situation on "the cowardice of the rest of the Greeks," referring to his long struggle in the 340s to rally opposition to Philip. He had harangued Athenians at that time, but here he absolved them, making clear that *others* had let Philip grow too great to defeat. He addressed, obliquely, the Battle of Chaeronea, a shadow still hanging over him fifteen years later. "When Luck, both inescapable and unfeeling, decided the struggle over the freedom of the Greeks — a battle that *you* fought — in the way that she wished and not as was just, not even in that situation did I abandon my loyalty toward you, or take anything in exchange for it — not favor, not hope of gain, not wealth, not power, not personal safety."[6]

Again looking back to the era of Philip, Demosthenes made the case that only he, of those who had dealt with the king, had been impervious to bribes. "I do not shrink from writing to you here," he boasted, "that although Philip was the most skilled of anyone in the entire span of human memory . . . at corrupting with money the leading men in each of the Greek cities, I alone was not vanquished. . . . I declined a lot of money that he tried to give, as many men now living are aware."[7] Demosthenes did not name the witnesses of his probity, and of course Aeschines, who was still alive but in exile, had testified numerous times to the opposite. But he maintained that a cadre of his supporters in Athens, and in all the cities of Greece, was looking on in dismay at the way the demos was treating him.

The letter insists on the spotlessness of Demosthenes' record of service, but it mostly avoids specifics. There were few episodes he could cite without raising troubling questions in the minds of his hearers. The winning of the Theban alliance, which he so proudly touted in earlier speeches, went unmentioned, for it had led to the twin disasters of Chaeronea and the destruction of Thebes. Demosthenes instead recurred to an event twenty years in the past, an Assembly showdown of 343, when the Peace of Philocrates was in effect but its terms were open to renegotiation. In that year Philip had sent a renowned orator, Python of Byzantium, to show the Assembly that Athens, not Macedon, was in the wrong; Demosthenes had countered Python's speech and restored civic pride. In recalling this episode he tried to summon respect for his eloquence, since his policies did not always do him credit.

"My present afflictions are so numerous, I'm at a loss as to which I should first lament," Demosthenes continued, turning to a different approach, hand-wringing. "Will it be the time of life at which I am compelled to go into a dangerous exile, contrary to custom and to what I deserve? Or the shame I've incurred after being convicted and ruined, without any evidence or disclosure? Or the hopes I am cheated of, instead getting woes that rightfully should have fallen to other men?"[8] He made the point, a valid one, that as the first to be tried he had been a target for anger directed at *all* the accused. Those who came later had mounted the same defense as he had, yet had won acquittal or later exoneration.

In a delicate stretch of the letter Demosthenes addressed his flight from Athens after his conviction, an act that in some eyes might have suggested guilt. He adduced his age as a reason for his escape, saying he could not survive the ordeal of prison. Then he pointed out that he had only run to a nearby place, Troezen, and then to a place even closer to Athens, Calauria. "From here, every day, I look across to my homeland."⁹ He had declined to go to Macedon and join with the enemy, though other leaders, including Themistocles, had sold out to foreign powers when they were exiled. He had stayed nearby, within sight of his native soil, to show his loyalty. This strategy was about to pay off handsomely.

In his parting words Demosthenes addressed himself to Hyperides and the others who had helped gain his conviction. "I wish to speak in particular to those who are knocking me down in front of you all," he wrote, aware that these men would oppose his return if they feared retribution. He offered an olive branch: in his eyes the prosecutors had acted as public servants and not from ill-will; hence he could forgive them.

"I level no charge," he promised, using a term that often refers to the filing of legal complaints. He claimed to want to be reconciled with his foes, but if this were not possible, then the demos must at least vote them down. "Don't let the hatred of these men have greater sway than your *charis* toward me," he concluded, using a complex word that conveyed gratitude, kindness, and favor. "Farewell."¹⁰

Whether "Concerning His Own Return" was ever read out in the Assembly or if so, how it was received, is not known. The letter may have been swept away by the flood of events and debates that seized the attention of Athens in midsummer 323, along with that of all the cities of Greece. Reports arrived from travelers leaving Babylon that Alexander had died there in early June, a victim, as was commonly (but probably wrongly) thought, of a poisoning scheme. Demosthenes likely had not received advance word, as he had done when Philip was killed, but rather learned the earthshaking news along with the rest of Greece as it galloped from Asia to Europe. In an instant, everything changed.

Athens was ready for just such a moment, with its pool of Harpalus money and the recruits marshaled by its general, Leosthenes. Nonetheless, voices of caution were raised in Assembly sessions, especially by the circumspect Phocion. "If Alexander is dead today, he'll still be dead tomorrow, and the day after that," Phocion told the Assembly. "We can take our decisions *then* and not make mistakes."[11] His partisans, the wealthy elite, had prospered in Alexander's empire and did not want to leave it; they opposed the move toward revolt. But those who followed Hyperides, including the poorer classes, had long been itching for war, and they had the majority.

Demosthenes had been on first one side, then the other, of the divide between the two factions. As a moderate he could help close the gap by talking to both sides at once, by way of a letter. At the same time he could reestablish his credit with the resisters, who had cause to doubt his allegiance. Both strategies might help him get back home, though he risked seeming selfish if he agitated for a recall when Athens was pressing ahead with a major war. Thus he began his letter "On Political Harmony" by putting aside his own exoneration. "Regarding my homeward arrival, I think you all will be able to plan about that at any time," he reassured the demos, "so I have written nothing about that on the present occasion."[12] Even so, the letter addresses concerns indirectly that bear on the topic.

Demosthenes expounded upon the danger he foresaw for Athens, though he kept his language vague and oblique. Those who had sided with Macedon might now fear reprisals from those who had not and cling the more closely to Antipater. What was needed was amnesty for the collaborators in order to create a united front in the war to come. "I say that you must not in any way cast blame, or chastise anyone, neither general nor orator nor private citizen, who seems to have acted in league with the established order," he wrote, using a cautious phrase to refer to collusion. "Rather you must concede to all that they have conducted their political role as was appropriate." The letter continues by deploying the time-honored metaphor of the ship of state. "You must think that, just as on a ship, when some recommend getting to safety by means of sails, and others by oars, that all of what's spoken by both is aimed at salvation."[13]

In case anyone missed the relevance to his own case of his amnesty proposal, Demosthenes made the point explicit. "I urge this course on you," he wrote, "though I myself have not received this kind of humane treatment from some, but have been unjustly and factiously tossed away, in order to please others." By these unnamed "others," Demosthenes was referring to the Macedonians, repeating the claim he made in an earlier letter (and doubtless at his trial): his indictment had been a sop to those masters. Lest he now seem to be harboring grudges, however, he quickly changed tack: "But I think I have not the right to harm the common good by indulging a private anger, and I do not mingle my personal hatred with the common goods." He vowed to practice himself the clemency that he preached.[14]

Because he was urging war against Macedon, Demosthenes knew that he risked awakening ghosts of the past, especially the disaster at Chaeronea. He was careful to characterize his advice as political, not military, and promised that he would not play armchair general. Along the way he delicately, and obliquely, inserted yet another defense of the Chaeronea debacle. "It is a very difficult position, giving advice, because things that have been correctly planned and assessed, with great toil and effort, are often ruined by those in authority making wrong use of them."[15] He was speaking of the current moment but clearly adverted to the past, when, as he had claimed in his funeral speech, bad Theban leadership, and bad luck, had doomed the Greek cause.

Luck had been against the Greeks for decades and had especially favored Alexander, Demosthenes concluded. "But now that Alexander is dead, Luck is looking for someone to partner with; you must be those people!" His final sentence exhorted the Athenians, "With luck on your side, free the Greeks!"[16]

Demosthenes' rallying cry echoed many speeches he'd given, and actions he'd taken, over the preceding thirty years. If these are indeed his last preserved words (as I here assume), they form a fitting finale to his career as an orator, a life spent wielding the Greek language with consummate skill, sometimes as a precision tool, at other times as a bludgeon.

"Freeing the Greeks" was exactly what the Athenians aimed to do. They sent their commander, Leosthenes, north with a powerful army to engage Antipater near Thermopylae and at the same time sent diplomats out to proclaim a Hellenic War. (Modern historians have renamed this conflict, calling it the Lamian War after the city, Lamia, where much of the action took place.)

"Hellenic War" implied that the conflict pitted Greeks against non-Greeks, but for many who heard the Athenian call to arms, the lines were not so sharp or loyalties predetermined. Some states took the field with Athens, while others, especially the cities of Boeotia and the Peloponnese, stayed loyal to Macedon and declined to join the Greek side. Hyperides led the effort to bring in more allies for Athens, while Antipater sent out his own envoys to try to deter defections. He made use of the Athenian orator Pytheas, one of the ten who'd prosecuted Demosthenes the previous year; Pytheas had since fled Athens and was now lending his talents to the Macedonian cause.

It was this Pytheas who had once insulted Demosthenes' speeches by saying they "smelled of the lamp," that is, were composed laboriously, late at night, when oil lamps burned. Demosthenes had retorted, "The lamp sees different things in your case and mine, Pytheas," implying that his detractor, a man half his age, was doing scandalous things in the night.[17] A deep animosity sprang up between these two, as we can judge by an oddly embittered passage in Demosthenes' letter "Concerning Lycurgus's Sons." Though elsewhere in his letters he refrained from ad hominem attacks, Demosthenes lashed out, uniquely, at Pytheas. He pointed out that Pytheas had risen from abject poverty to great wealth, presumably the result of taking bribes. "He's doing so well he can keep two courtesans, who are kind enough to accompany him as he heads toward death from consumption," Demosthenes wrote.[18]

Watching from exile the diplomatic contest between Pytheas, speaking for Macedon, and Hyperides, speaking for Athens, Demosthenes saw that his own oratory might tip the scales. Once before, at a similar juncture, he had brought Thebes over to the side of Athens by force of words (by his own account), when Philip's best speakers were ranged on the opposite side. Perhaps he could pull off a similar coup in the Peloponnese, the region that lay a short hop from Calauria. Without authorization from Athens, without even regaining his citizen rights, he left his island refuge and made an impromptu diplomatic tour, advocating the cause of Hellenic freedom. He came face-to-face with Pytheas in Arcadia, and according to Plutarch bested him there in a verbal duel before the Ten Thousand, the region's deliberative body.[19]

Demosthenes had further successes in other Peloponnesian cities, including Corinth. According to one source, he teamed up with his former ally, then briefly his foe, now his ally again: Hyperides. He is said to have seconded or supported his friend in diplomatic debates. (Another source says he played this tag-team role with a different envoy.)

Back in Athens, the Assembly got word of Demosthenes' efforts and voted at last to exonerate him, even sending a warship to fetch him home. After nearly a year in exile, after all his wheedling, pleading letters had failed, after his former friends had declined to come to his aid, Demosthenes had found his way back into favor. His eloquence had restored his civic stature.

Huge crowds gathered to cheer as Demosthenes landed in Piraeus and made the long walk to the city. He paused as he walked and raised his hands to the sky in thanks to the gods, grateful that he had made a peaceful return from exile, in contrast to those who had forced their way back in. Soon afterward, on the proposal of his cousin Demon, the Assembly remitted his fifty-talent fine, voting him into a ceremonial office and setting his pay at precisely fifty talents.

Far to the north, the Hellenic War was on a favorable footing. The Athenian-led Greek army had forced Antipater's forces into a weak position, under siege in the city of Lamia and running short of supplies. Antipater had even tried to surrender on terms, but Leosthenes had refused, anticipating a total victory.

Demosthenes could look ahead to the future that Hyperides had spoken of the previous year as something forever lost. "We could have had the greatest prestige among the demos," Hyperides had lamented, referring to himself and Demosthenes. Now it appeared that the two would gain that prestige after all, and Demosthenes would see his mistakes and bad luck, and the failure of Chaeronea, redeemed at last.

CHAPTER TWELVE

I Depart from Your Shrine Still Alive

I n Athens, Demosthenes was reunited with family and friends –
what few friends had stayed loyal. His two sons were now
perhaps in their teens; they probably had not accompanied him into
exile, though it is noteworthy that he says nothing about separation
from them, or from his wife, in his letters pleading for restoration,
beyond a vague reference to being deprived of "the company of my
dear ones." His nephew Demochares, now making his own way as a
public speaker, was presumably glad to have him back, though another nephew, Phrynion, may have felt otherwise. Phrynion, brother
of Demochares, is known to us as a cad thanks to a legal speech
preserved in the works of Demosthenes but almost certainly not by
him. According to that speech Phrynion treated Neaira, his courtesan, with a terrible lack of respect, forcing her to have sex in public
to demonstrate his hold over her. She ran away from him in disgust. [1]

Demosthenes too was linked by gossip with a courtesan, the
famous Laïs, a woman who modeled her beautiful breasts for paint-
ers depicting goddesses. If he was indeed her lover, he shared that
distinction with Aristippus of Cyrene, his polar opposite in lifestyle

and mores. Aristippus was an apostle of hedonism, a philosopher who preached that pleasure was the only human good, whereas Demosthenes was abstemious to a fault, mocked by his peers for drinking water, not wine. But Laïs was famous for the diversity of her clients. She reportedly gave her favors gratis to Diogenes the Cynic, who had stripped himself of home, property, and social status in order to gain perfect freedom.

Perhaps there was a young man in Athens, an athletic youth of rare beauty, whom Demosthenes was glad to see once again. The essay titled "Erotikos" in Greek, indicating that it deals with sexual love, is framed as a speech of advice addressed to this youth, Epicrates, by an older man who is clearly in love with him. The speaker, however, declines to pursue a sexual liaison; his goal is to turn Epicrates toward "philosophy," a term that in this context means little more than serious ethical thought. "Erotikos" is preserved among the works of Demosthenes, and we have no good reason to doubt the attribution, though it has often been questioned. What led Demosthenes to compose such an essay, if indeed it is his, is a matter for speculation; it is the only work in his corpus not meant for public delivery, and also the only one that deals with amatory emotions.

Among the speakers active in politics, few can have been happy to see Demosthenes back. Demades, who had once helped him evade extradition by Alexander, had apparently become contemptuous; a speech composed by someone impersonating Demades, perhaps recalling things he had actually said, referred to Demosthenes as a "homunculus made up of syllables and tongue." Phocion was no friend of Demosthenes either. The two men had long been at odds over policy toward Macedon, leading to an exchange preserved by Plutarch. Demosthenes reportedly told the cautious, conservative Phocion, "If the Athenians ever lose their minds, they will kill you," to which Phocion replied, "And when they regain their sanity, they'll kill *you*."[2] Phocion opposed the Hellenic War on the grounds that Athens did not have the strength to win it.

Another Athenian who must have been dismayed at Demosthenes' return was a man named Theramenes, who, to judge by one of Demosthenes' letters ("On the Slanders of Theramenes," which is considered genuine but less confidently than the letters discussed above), had made the case in public that Demosthenes was cursed and brought bad luck with him wherever he went. In the letter, Demosthenes protests that Athens has had much *good* luck in recent years, then hits back at his detractor with by now familiar jabs. "He [Theramenes] is a friend to the whore Pausanias," the letter concludes, "and though he shows the bravado of a man, he gets used like a woman."[3] Demosthenes knew how much *that* barb could sting, having felt it himself in his clashes with Aeschines.

The firmest ally Demosthenes still had was Hyperides. The Harpalus affair had dealt a huge blow to their friendship, but at this moment the two were aligned on the need to press the war vigorously. Hyperides had full confidence in Leosthenes, the general besieging Antipater's forces, and Demosthenes, for his part, had vowed not to interfere in strategy. The siege cordon around Antipater's forces seemed to be holding, but reports from the front evidently gave cause for concern. A very short letter tentatively attributed to Demosthenes relates that both the Greek and Macedonian sides were claiming recent successes and reassured the Assembly that all was well. The letter serves as a cover note to a longer eyewitness account that has not been preserved, purportedly sent by one of Leosthenes' soldiers.[4]

All might have been well but for a stroke of the same bad luck that had often dogged Demosthenes. While skirmishing too close to the walls of Lamia, Leosthenes was hit in the head by a slinger's shot; the wound proved fatal. Other commanders took over, but the army's morale was shaken, and some contingents opted to leave and go home rather than stay the winter in rugged quarters. The numbers in the Greek coalition diminished.

As they had done previously, after Chaeronea and during other wars, the Athenians held a solemn ceremony to inter the war dead, appointing a civic leader to give the eulogy. Hyperides was chosen for the high-profile, highly prestigious assignment; Demosthenes' reputation had been too badly tarnished. A portion of the funeral oration has survived in yet another papyrus find of the mid-1800s. Unusually, it glorified a single, named individual, Leosthenes, while bestowing blanket praise on all the dead and asserting the rightness of the cause for which they had died — "the freedom of the Greeks." Were it not for their sacrifice, the speech proclaims, "the entire inhabited world would be under one master, and Greece would be compelled to treat its decisions as law."[5] Hyperides spoke as though those prospects had already been prevented, but the outcome of the war still hung in the balance.

In Lamia, Antipater's men were running out of supplies, but relief arrived just in time. A force led by one of Alexander's generals, Leonnatus, crossed over from Asia to Europe to break the siege, and though Leonnatus was killed in a battle against the Greek forces, he drew enough troops away from the cordon to let those trapped within break free.

The war then took on a different cast, and, within a few months it was over. At Crannon, in Thessaly, in August 322, the Greek coalition lost an open-field battle to Antipater's replenished forces. Though their casualties were light, the Greeks surrendered the following day and conceded, as before, the loss of their freedom. The "one master" Hyperides had reviled was in full control of Greece, of

Athens, and of the fates of all who had stirred the rebellion, including Demosthenes.

For thirty years Macedon had tried not to meddle in the internal affairs of Athens, at least not openly. Philip's hope and that of his son Alexander was that Athens would come over willingly to the new Macedonian order, becoming a partner (albeit a subordinate one) rather than a subject. Antipater had no use for that plan. He had been cooped up in Lamia for months and nearly starved to death; the license he had given to Athens had been repaid with scorn and defiance. As he brought his army south, he let it be known that the price imposed on Athens would be steep, and would include the surrender of Demosthenes, along with other orators who had supported the war.

When Alexander had made the same demand after the fall of Thebes, thirteen years earlier, Phocion and Demades had managed to win clemency for those on the wanted list. The same two envoys were sent to Antipater after the Battle of Crannon, but the result was different this time. Antipater was not in the mood to compromise. He insisted on installing a garrison in Piraeus to ensure that Athens stayed loyal; the will of Macedon would henceforth be backed up by armed force. The poor of Athens, the greatest supporters of the war, would be disenfranchised, and only the rich and well-off, about nine thousand men, would have the right to hold office or vote. The speakers on his enemies list would have to be handed over.

Demosthenes did not bother to ask for the Assembly's protection or tell pointed stories of sheep protected by dogs. When he heard that Antipater sought his life, he fled Athens, along with Hyperides and two or three other opponents of Macedon. In his absence, his nephew Demochares made a bold show of support, rising to speak on his uncle's behalf with a sword girt around his waist.

The idea of defying Antipater, though, was swiftly rejected. On the motion of Demades, the demos condemned both Demosthenes and Hyperides to death, a decree that gave Antipater legal cover to hunt the men down and destroy them. For good measure, the Assembly added a clause that forbade the burial of their remains in Athenian soil.

The two condemned men, together with allies, sailed to the island of Aegina and there parted ways. Hyperides and the others took refuge in a sanctuary devoted to Aeacus, a mythic hero thought to have reigned on the island. They could hope that the demigod's power might protect them, or at least inspire shame in their pursuers, who would have to break religious taboos in order to extract them. Demosthenes held out similar hopes for a place he knew from his time in exile, the shrine of Poseidon on Calauria. He said his farewells to Hyperides and pressed onward, no doubt assuming that Antipater's toughest agents were not far behind.

Antipater had chosen a man named Archias, a former tragic actor turned bounty hunter, to bring in the wanted men. Archias had perhaps already earned his epithet *phugadotheras*, "exile-chaser," or perhaps he received it on account of this, his most famous mission. Aiding him on his hunt was a gang of Thracian mercenaries, warriors known for their toughness and savagery. As non-Greeks, they worshipped neither Aeacus nor Poseidon, a point that recommended them for the jobs they now had to do.

The squad went first to Aegina in pursuit of Hyperides and his comrades. Our best report of what happened next is confusing; evidently enmeshing the story with that of Demosthenes, it places the men in a shrine of Poseidon, not Aeacus. The report paints a piteous picture of Hyperides wrapping his arms around the god's statue as his captors drag him away.[6] His hope of finding safety through contact with the divine had come to nothing.

Hyperides was conveyed to Antipater, either at Corinth or a nearby town called Cleonae. There he was tortured and, by one report, bit off his tongue so as not to reveal state secrets; more likely, as another account says, Antipater cut out his tongue to teach the Greeks the cost of freedom of speech. In a further punishment straight out of myth, his body was cast out on the ground, unburied, to be desecrated by eaters of carrion. In Sophocles' *Antigone,* and other plays on the same theme, an autocrat, Creon, leaves the body of his foe, Polynices, unburied, but no one had imitated in life what had been portrayed in art. A family friend, we are told, contrived to have Hyperides' body cremated and the ashes sent back to Athens, where they were secretly interred in violation of the Assembly's decree.

"Exile-chaser" Archias moved on to Calauria in search of Demosthenes. Plutarch describes what happened next in vivid detail, though he also admits that the sources he consulted differed somewhat. Inevitably, he selected the versions he found most dramatic, including one that gave an account — most likely invented, but meaningful nevertheless — of a dream Demosthenes had on his last night on earth.[7]

According to Plutarch, Demosthenes dreamed that he and Archias were both performing in tragedies, at the yearly festival where, in Athens, playwrights competed to win the prize for best play. In the dream, Demosthenes felt that he had given a good performance and won over the audience. But he lost to Archias regardless, because the production's *choregia* — costumes, equipment and training provided by a wealthy patron — had fallen short. The dream makes use of episodes from the orator's life to give new dimensions to his imminent death. Demosthenes had first learned to speak effectively when tutored by a tragic actor, Satyrus; later his own choregia had been sabotaged by his enemy Meidias. In the dream he lays claim to superior talent even while losing his prize due to factors outside his control. He gains a moral victory in defeat, just as he claimed that Athens had done in the Battle of Chaeronea.

On the morning after this dream, Plutarch wrote, Archias and his Thracians landed on Calauria, then made their way to the shrine of Poseidon, where Demosthenes had gone as a suppliant. Leaving his spearmen to guard the entrance, Archias went inside and spoke kind words to Demosthenes, who was seated near the cult image of Poseidon. He told his quarry that if he came willingly, Antipater would do him no harm. Demosthenes replied with a quip relating to the dream he had had. "Archias," he retorted, "in the past you never convinced me with your acting, and you won't convince me now with your promises." Archias grew angry and started issuing threats, prompting another joke from Demosthenes, that the actor had now doffed his mask and was speaking the truth.[8]

Two sources differ on how events played out. One says that Archias tried to use force to tear Demosthenes away, but local people prevented it—a stirring act of defiance, if true. Demosthenes then remarked, perhaps in an effort to defuse the conflict, that he had entered the shrine not to preserve his life but to force Macedon to display its contempt for the gods.[9] Plutarch, our other ancient source, mentions none of these details, but depicts the exchange between Archias and Demosthenes as civil and nonviolent throughout. Demosthenes, he recounts, asked for leave to compose a message to the people of Athens, implying that he would go with Archias when that was done. Archias gave his consent, and Demosthenes withdrew inside the temple and took up a papyrus scroll. He put the end of his writing stylus in his mouth as though thinking. Then he covered his head with his cloak.

In Plutarch's account, Demosthenes had hidden a fast-acting

poison inside the stylus, then sucked it out when he seemed to be writing his letter. But ancient authors were fascinated by this suicide story and told it in various ways. Some said the poison was hidden in a bracelet, others in a ring, still others wrapped up in a piece of Demosthenes' clothing. Whatever the case, Demosthenes had clearly planned ahead for this moment, determined to die a free man and on his own terms.

None of the troops in the arrest posse was as yet aware of what had just happened. As the toxin took effect and Demosthenes let his head droop, the Thracian guards looking on made fun of him as a weak man, thinking he had swooned in the face of danger. Archias came over and made one more effort to lead him away, saying again that Antipater would not harm him. Demosthenes, confident now that death was at hand, ventured a third quip concerning his captor's former acting career. "If you play the part of Creon and cast my body out unburied, you would not be getting ahead of yourself," he said, implying, to the no doubt mystified Archias, that he was already a corpse.

Then Demosthenes turned to the statue of Poseidon at the rear of the temple. "My dear Poseidon," he said, "I depart from your shrine still alive, though not even your sacred precinct has been left undefiled by Antipater and the Macedonians." He had made up his mind to go into the open air while he still had strength, since dying in the god's dwelling would pollute it. His pursuers helped him to his feet and supported him as he stumbled past the altar, but there the poison overcame him. He slumped to the ground, and with a final groan, he was dead.

So runs the story of Demosthenes' end, as selected by Plutarch from out of "very many" versions extant in his day. Before concluding the tale, Plutarch paused to note one final divergent account. Demochares, Demosthenes' nephew, denied that his uncle used poison or took his own life. He insisted that the gods intervened to grant a noble and painless death to Demosthenes, at the moment he needed a route of escape.[10] This was one of the lifelong efforts Demochares made to repair his uncle's image and burnish his legacy — efforts at which he succeeded, as will be explored in the Epilogue.

The papyrus before which Demosthenes spent his last minutes was later examined and found to contain the heading of a letter: "Demosthenes to Antipater." There was nothing else on it. The last written work of the ultimate master of words, who toiled over speeches by lamplight while others were drinking wine at parties and banquets, was a nearly blank page. Thus ended the life of Demosthenes, leader of Athens.

Epilogue

IF YOU'D HAD STRENGTH
TO EQUAL YOUR JUDGMENT

The upheavals that had, in the space of a year, led to Demosthenes being kicked out of Athens, then welcomed back, then kicked out again and condemned to death continued to trouble Athens in subsequent years. Soon after Demosthenes' suicide, the two Athenian leaders who had overseen his destruction, Phocion and Demades, were also executed, as the factions to which they belonged fell from favor or power. Athens had by then become an objective for both sides in a Macedonian civil war; as the struggle see-sawed, so did the city's politics, at one time oligarchic, then democratic, then oligarchic again. Amid the confusion, many Athenians built a personality cult around a Macedonian strongman, the warlord Demetrius, who promised them stability and protection.

A lone voice raised against the Demetrius cult was that of Demochares, Demosthenes' nephew. Demochares saw himself as the heir of his uncle's leadership role and political values, especially of his commitment to freedom of speech and the sovereignty of the Assembly. Just as he had once stood at the bema wearing a sword at his waist, so in the age of Demetrius he ridiculed those who toadied to the warlord or accepted his gifts and preferments. As a result the Assembly, controlled by the warlord's allies, banished him from Athens as the fourth century drew to a close. He spent some fifteen years in exile but returned in 287, after the city had kicked Demetrius out and become democratic again. As one of the few still untainted by collusion with despotism, Demochares stood high in the esteem of the demos.

Six or seven years later, Demochares drew on his standing to propose public honors for his uncle, including a bronze statue in the marketplace and, for Demosthenes' sons, the privilege of *sitesis*, the right to take meals in a state dining hall reserved for high officials. Forty years had passed since Demosthenes' death, and the view of the demos had softened, especially since those decades had brought the city much misery. Political life had deteriorated; during the reign of Demetrius, many Athenians had cravenly worshipped their warlord as a god. Against that backdrop, the legacy of Demosthenes, a man who stood up to an earlier strongman, Philip, took on a new luster.

By chance the decree that Demochares moved, proposing commemorations of his uncle's civic service, has been preserved among works ascribed to Plutarch.[1] In it Demochares backed up his motion by recounting Demosthenes' benefactions. He included a list of his uncle's bequests of money: to subsidize a military campaign in Euboea, to outfit warships, to ransom prisoners, to subsidize a choral performance, to buy weapons for soldiers who lacked them, to repair the defenses of Piraeus, and — a fact not known from other sources — to feed the needy during a shortage of grain. The last item doubtless hit home with the demos, for Athens had suffered two terrible famines within recent years when warfare had cut off supplies.

Demochares then turned to his uncle's political record, highlighting only one episode in a long and, it's fair to say, checkered career. "He brought over into alliance with the demos . . . the Thebans, Euboeans, Corinthians, Megarians, Achaeans, Locrians, Byzantines, and Messenians, and amassed forces for the demos and for our allies: ten thousand foot soldiers and a thousand cavalrymen." The numbers and list of contributing states suggest the Hellenic/Lamian War, but the inclusion of Thebans also recalls Chaeronea. On the subject of the Harpalus affair and the bribery scandal, the decree is silent.

The Assembly passed Demochares' proposal. A bronze statue of Demosthenes was commissioned from one Polyeuctus, a relative unknown but, to judge by the work he created, a master of portraiture. Three Roman copies of the life-size statue have been recovered in modern times, as well as some fifty busts that were clearly derived from it. The same careworn face appears on them all: knit brows, downcast eyes, tight-set mouth. The hollow cheeks bespeak the life of a "water-drinker," a man who eschewed wine and social occasions to labor over his writing. The body, partly exposed by the fall of the mantle, shows age but also strength. The hands, in the copies we have, grip a tightly furled scroll, perhaps a speech or a legal writ, but this was a Roman alteration; the bronze original, as we know from Plutarch, depicted the hands clasped together.

The statue was set up near the Altar of the Twelve Gods in the Athenian Agora, next to an impressive plane tree and a place called the *perischoinisma*, "roped-off area," whose use is unknown. At some point more than a century later, a rueful poem was inscribed on the pedestal, in elegiac verse form: "Demosthenes, if you'd had strength to equal your judgment, / Macedonian Ares would never have ruled the Greeks." According to one source, Demosthenes had written those lines himself as he waited in the shrine of Poseidon for poison to end his life, but almost certainly some anonymous poet composed them long afterward.[2]

By that time the Greeks had fallen under the rule of the Roman Empire, so the inscription carried an extra layer of meaning. A second "barbarian" power had subjugated Hellas; no Athenian leader had been able to stand against the tide of history. "The freedom of the Greeks," a catch phrase for the autonomous city-state culture that defined Greece's classical age, could not be raised up again once it had been thrown down at the battles of Chaeronea and Crannon.

Another century after that poem was inscribed, in the late first century CE, Plutarch saw the statue during a visit to Athens and heard an intriguing story about it. It seems that a soldier who had been summoned to a legal proceeding, needing to quickly hide some gold that he carried, stuck it in the first hiding place he could find — the statue's clasped hands. Leaves from the nearby plane tree covered the gold so that it went unnoticed by passersby. After a time, the soldier returned to find that his wealth, hidden under the leaves, had not been disturbed. The tale of the unstolen treasure was making the rounds in Athens when Plutarch arrived, and the city's wits were turning out epigrams on how Demosthenes had in the end proven immune to bribes.[3]

Plutarch says that the wind that blew the leaves over the gold arose "from chance [ek tyches]," though he also concedes that the soldier may have placed the leaves there himself. His primary explanation was framed in significant language. It was Tyche, in the sense of *bad* luck, which, Demosthenes always maintained, had foiled his plans to save Athens and had led to the defeat at Chaeronea. His enemies had cast *him* as bad luck personified, an accursed figure who ruined whatever he touched.

Epilogue

Four centuries after his conviction on charges of graft, Demosthenes had been exonerated, Plutarch averred, thanks to the workings of tyche. Far too late to preserve Athenian freedom or protect democracy, too late to save Thebes from annihilation, but not too late to clear his own name in the annals of history, Demosthenes' run of bad luck had finally turned.

Chronology

All dates are BCE; speeches not otherwise attributed are by Demosthenes.

404	Defeat of Athens by Sparta in the Peloponnesian War
385 or 384	Birth of Demosthenes in Athens
376	Death of Demosthenes' father
364	Demosthenes launches his speaking career with lawsuits against his guardians; "Against Aphobus 1"
359	Philip II becomes king of Macedon
357	Philip besieges and captures Amphipolis; Athens declares war on Philip
356	Birth of Alexander (later called the Great); Phocians' seizure of Delphi leads to the Third Sacred War
355	Social War (revolt of Aegean states from Athens)
354	"On the Naval Boards"
353 or 352	Possible date of "On the Rhodians' Freedom"
351	"First Philippic"
349	Philip campaigns in the Chalcidice; "First Olynthiac," "Second Olynthiac"
348	"Third Olynthiac"; Olynthus destroyed by Philip
347	"Against Meidias"
346	Athenian negotiations with Philip produce the Peace of Philocrates; Demosthenes serves as ambassador to Philip; end of Third Sacred War
345	Demosthenes indicts Aeschines for "false embassy" on missions to Philip; Aeschines counters with "Against Timarchus"
344	"Second Philippic"
343	Demosthenes' suit against Aeschines comes to trial; Aeschines and Demosthenes each deliver a speech "On the False Embassy"; Aeschines acquitted by a narrow margin
341	"On the Chersonese," "Third Philippic"

Chronology

340	Demosthenes awarded a crown for service to Athens; Philip moves against Perinthus and Byzantium, seizes Athenian grain ships
339	Fourth Sacred War begins; Philip seizes Elateia in central Greece; Athens concludes an alliance with Thebes against Philip
338	Athenian-Theban defeat at Battle of Chaeronea; Demosthenes delivers oration over war dead; Philip founds League of Corinth
336	Philip assassinated; Alexander becomes king of Macedon; Aeschines brings suit against Ctesiphon for proposing a crown for Demosthenes
335	Theban revolt, spurred by Demosthenes, results in annihilation of Thebes
334	Start of Alexander's Asian campaign
330	Aeschines' suit against Ctesiphon goes to trial; Aeschines delivers "Against Ctesiphon," Demosthenes counters with "On the Crown"; Aeschines goes into exile after losing the case
324	Alexander issues Exiles Decree; Harpalus arrives in Athens; bribery charges brought against Demosthenes
323	Trial and conviction of Demosthenes; Demosthenes writes letters from exile; Alexander dies in Babylon (June); Athens leads a revolt against Macedonian forces; Demosthenes returns from exile after supporting the Athenian cause from abroad
322	Greek defeat at the Battle of Crannon; flight of Hyperides and Demosthenes; death of Demosthenes on Calauria
c. 280	Urged by Demochares, Athens erects honorific statue of Demosthenes

Source Notes

CHAPTER 1. I ALONE WILL BE SHOWN TO HAVE SPOKEN THE TRUTH

Ernst Badian examines Demosthenes' early history in "The Road to Prominence," in Worthington, *Demosthenes: Statesman and Orator*, 9–44, and in the same volume David Mirhady discusses Demosthenes' suits against the guardians ("Demosthenes as Advocate: The Private Speeches," 186–198). The speech "Against Aphobus 1" is translated and annotated by D. M. MacDowell in *Demosthenes, Speeches 27 and 28;* annotations to the Greek text by Lionel Pearson can be found in *Demosthenes: Six Private Speeches* (Norman: University of Oklahoma Press, 1972). An annotated translation of the speech "On the Naval Boards" (also known as "On the Symmories") is available in *Demosthenes, Speeches 1–17.*

CHAPTER 2. *THAT* WAS THE CRITICAL MOMENT

Annotated translations of the speeches "On the Rhodians' Freedom" and "First Philippic" are available in *Demosthenes, Speeches 1–17.* The "First Philippic" has been the focus of much inquiry and commentary; see especially C. W. Wooten, *A Commentary on Demosthenes' Philippic I* (Oxford: Oxford University Press, 2008). In addition the "First Philippic" forms part of two composite commentaries that also include the three Olynthiac speeches dealt with in Chapter 3: J. E. Sandys, *The First Philippic and the Olynthiacs of Demosthenes* (London: Macmillan, 1897), and, more recently, Judson Herrmann, *Demosthenes: Selected Political Speeches* (Cambridge: Cambridge University Press, 2019).

CHAPTER 3. WHEN WILL YOU DO WHAT IS NEEDED, IF NOT NOW?

The Olynthiac speeches are translated and annotated in *Demosthenes, Speeches 1–17;* commentaries on the Greek text can be found in J. E. Sandys, *The First Philippic and the Olynthiacs of Demosthenes* (London: Macmillan, 1897), and Judson Herrmann, *Demosthenes: Selected Political Speeches* (Cambridge: Cambridge University Press, 2019), as well as in E. I. McQueen, *Demosthenes' Olynthiacs* (London: Bristol Classical Press, 1986). There is dispute over whether Demosthenes proposed, in the "Third Olynthiac," to divert money from the Theoric Fund; see in particular E. M. Harris, "Demosthenes and the Theoric Fund," in Harris, ed., *Transitions to Empire: Essays in Honor of E. Badian,* 59–76 (Norman: University of Oklahoma Press, 1996). The speech "Against

Meidias" has been translated and annotated by E. M. Harris in *Demosthenes: Speeches 20–22* (Austin: University of Texas Press, 2008); commentary on Greek text can be found in Douglas M. MacDowell, *Demosthenes: Against Meidias* (Oxford: Oxford University Press, 1990).

CHAPTER 4. NONE OF US WAS WILLING TO DINE WITH HIM

On Aeschines of Sphettus see Harris, *Aeschines and Athenian Politics*. The three surviving speeches are translated and annotated by Chris Carey in *Aeschines*. The speech "Against Timarchus" has received a more extensive commentary, together with a new English translation, in Nick Fisher's *Aeschines: Against Timarchus* (Oxford: Oxford University Press, 2001), a volume in the very useful Clarendon Ancient History series. The complex events of 346 and the start of the conflict between Aeschines and Demosthenes are made admirably intelligible by T. T. B. Ryder in section 2 of his "Demosthenes and Philip II," in Worthington, *Demosthenes; Statesman and Orator*, 58–72. See also John Buckler, "Demosthenes and Aeschines," chapter 4 in the same volume.

CHAPTER 5. YOU HAVEN'T BEEN DEFEATED, FOR YOU HAVEN'T SO MUCH AS STIRRED

Isocrates' "To Philip" is translated and annotated by Terry L. Papillon in *Isocrates II* (Austin: University of Texas Press, 2004), 74–108. Demosthenes' "Second Philippic," in which the speech made earlier in Messene is summarized, is found in translation in *Demosthenes, Speeches 1–17*, and in Greek with commentary in J. E. Sandys, *Demosthenes: On the Peace, Second Philippic, On the Chersonesus and Third Philippic* (London: Macmillan, 1900). His speech "On the False Embassy" is translated and annotated by Harvey Yunis in *Demosthenes, Speeches 18 and 19*; a commentary on the Greek text is in D. M. MacDowell, *Demosthenes: On the False Embassy (Oration 19)* (Oxford: Oxford University Press, 2000). Aeschines' speech of the same title is found in Chris Carey's *Aeschines*. Demosthenes' "On the Chersonese" and "Third Philippic" are extensively annotated in Sandys, *Demosthenes*, and Judson Herrmann, *Demosthenes: Selected Political Speeches* (Cambridge: Cambridge University Press, 2019); a translation and annotations are also in *Demosthenes, Speeches 1–17*.

CHAPTER 6. I ALONE DID NOT DESERT MY PLACE

The new powers of the Areopagus in Demosthenes' time are dealt with by Hansen in *The Athenian Democracy in the Age of Demosthenes*, chapter 12. The "Letter of Philip" and Demosthenes' "Response to the Letter of Philip" are translated and annotated in *Demosthenes, Speeches 1–17*. On Demosthenes' pro-Theban strategies in the period leading up to Chaeronea see George Cawkwell, "Demosthenes' Policy after the Peace of Philocrates," *Classical Quarterly* 13 (1963): 120–138 and 200–213.

Source Notes

The Battle of Chaeronea has been a subject of intense debate among historians; a forthcoming volume to be published by Peeters (Leuven, Belgium), collecting the papers delivered at the 2024 conference sponsored by the Museum of Cycladic Art, Athens (*Chaeronea, August 338: The State of the Question*, directed by Panagiotis Iossif), will present the results of the most up-to-date research, especially that of historians Peter Krentz and John Ma. Demosthenes' Funeral Oration (Speech 60) is translated and annotated by Ian Worthington in *Demosthenes, Speeches 60 and 61;* the same author defends the attribution of the speech to Demosthenes in "The Authorship of the Demosthenic *Epitaphios*," *Museum Helveticum* 60 (2003): 152–157. Isocrates' "To Philip 2" (Epistle 3) is included in Terry L. Papillon, *Isocrates II* (Austin: University of Texas Press, 2004).

The recovered fragments of Hyperides' "Against Diondas" were published by Chris Carey and a team of collaborators in "Fragments of Hyperides' *Against Diondas* from the Archimedes Palimpsest," *Zeitschrift für Papyrologie und Epigraphik* 165 (2008): 1–19. Analysis is found in S. C. Todd, "Hypereides' *Against Diondas,* Demosthenes' *On the Crown,* and the Rhetoric of Political Failure," and Judson Herrmann, "Hyperides' *Against Diondas* and the Rhetoric of Revolt," *Bulletin of the Institute for Classical Studies* 52 (2009): 161–174; 175–185.

The speech of Aeschines "Against Ctesiphon" is translated and annotated by Chris Carey in *Aeschines;* there is no recent English-language commentary on the Greek text. By contrast Demosthenes' "On the Crown" has been widely translated and annotated, for example in the volume by Yunis, *Demosthenes, Speeches 18 and 19;* Yunis has also produced a masterful commentary in *Demosthenes: On the Crown* (Cambridge: Cambridge University Press, 2008). Other recent commentaries include S. Usher, *Demosthenes: On the Crown* (Warminster: Aris and Phillips, 1993), and W. W. Goodwin, *Demosthenes: On the Crown* (Cambridge: Cambridge University Press, 1901, reprinted 1953).

Dinarchus's speech "Against Demosthenes" is translated and annotated by Ian Worthington in *Dinarchus, Hyperides, and Lycurgus;* the same author has produced a valuable commentary, *A Historical Commentary on Dinarchus: Rhetoric and Conspiracy in Fourth-Century Athens* (Ann Arbor: University of Michigan Press, 1994). Hyperides' "Against Demosthenes" is translated and annotated by Craig Cooper in *Dinarchus, Hyperides, and Lycurgus*. Friedrich Blass's edition of Hyperides, *Hyperidis Orationes Sex cum Ceterarum Fragmentis* (Leipzig: Teubner, 1894), has useful edits and comments.

CHAPTER 11. HIDE YOUR FACES FOR SHAME!

Jonathan Goldstein's *The Letters of Demosthenes* (New York: Columbia University Press, 1968) contains translations of all six letters, historical commentary, and extensive arguments for accepting three of the six as genuine (with a strong inclination toward the genuineness of a fourth). The letters can also be found, translated and annotated by Ian Worthington, in *Demosthenes, Speeches 60 and 61*. Worthington accepts Goldstein's arguments regarding Demosthenic authorship and goes farther by defending a short letter that Goldstein rejected: see Ian Worthington, "The Authenticity of Demosthenes' Sixth Letter," *Mnemosyne* 56 (2003): 585–589.

CHAPTER 12. I DEPART FROM YOUR SHRINE STILL ALIVE

Demosthenes' "Erotikos" is generally dismissed as non-Demosthenic, including by Worthington (*Demosthenes and the Fall of Classical Greece*, 29), but N. W. De Witt, the editor of the Loeb Classical Library volume containing the essay, notes that there are no linguistic grounds on which to dismiss it and reserves judgment (*Demosthenes, Orations 60–61, Funeral Speech, Erotic Essay, Exordia, Letters*, Loeb Classical Library 374 [Cambridge, Mass.: Harvard University Press, 1949], 40–41). The annotated and translated text can be found in *Demosthenes, Speeches 60 and 61*, translated by Worthington. Hyperides' Funeral Oration is translated and annotated by Judson Herrmann in *Hyperides: Funeral Oration* (Oxford: Oxford University Press, 2009), as well as by Craig Cooper in *Dinarchus, Hyperides, and Lycurgus*.

EPILOGUE

The complex history of post-Alexander Athens is surveyed by Christian Habicht, *Athens from Alexander to Anthony* (Cambridge, Mass.: Harvard University Press, 1997), and also figures prominently in my own earlier volume for the Ancient Lives series, *Demetrius: Sacker of Cities* (New Haven: Yale University Press, 2022).

Notes

All translations from the Greek are my own.

CHAPTER 1. I ALONE WILL BE SHOWN TO HAVE SPOKEN THE TRUTH

1. All dates are BCE.

2. Plutarch, *Demosthenes* 5.

3. Plutarch, *Demosthenes* 8.

4. Demosthenes 27.47–48 ("Against Aphobus 1").

5. [Plutarch,] *Lives of the Ten Orators* 844b–c.

6. See [Plutarch,] *Lives of the Ten Orators* 844b. In *Demosthenes* 5 Plutarch claims that Demosthenes could not afford to study with Isocrates.

7. For these various stratagems, see Plutarch, *Demosthenes* 7, 11.

8. See Plutarch, *Demosthenes* 7.

9. Demosthenes 14.24, 41 ("On the Naval Boards").

10. Demosthenes 15.6 ("On the Rhodians' Freedom").

CHAPTER 2. *THAT* WAS THE CRITICAL MOMENT

1. See Demosthenes 10.27 ("Fourth Philippic").

2. Demosthenes 1.9 ("First Olynthiac").

3. The date of the speech is disputed; it may have come as late as 351, though it is hard to believe that Demosthenes would have given Philip such short shrift if he had already delivered the "First Philippic."

4. Demosthenes 15.24 ("On the Rhodians' Freedom").

5. Demosthenes 15.17–18.

6. Demosthenes 15.19.

7. Demosthenes 4.1 ("First Philippic").

8. See Longinus, *On the Sublime* 18; Demosthenes 4.10–11.

9. Demosthenes 4.40.

10. Demosthenes 4.29.

11. Demosthenes 3.5 ("Third Olynthiac").

CHAPTER 3. WHEN WILL YOU DO WHAT IS NEEDED, IF NOT NOW?

1. Demosthenes 1.19 ("First Olynthiac").

2. Demosthenes 1.19–20.

3. Demosthenes 1.15.

4. Demosthenes 2.18–19 ("Second Olynthiac").

5. Demosthenes 2.10.

6. Demosthenes 2.1, 2.22.

7. Demosthenes 3.22 ("Third Olynthiac").

8. Demosthenes 3.31, 3.16.

9. Demosthenes 21.207 ("Against Meidias").

CHAPTER 4. NONE OF US WAS WILLING TO DINE WITH HIM

1. Aeschines 2.21, 2.34 ("On the False Embassy").

2. Aeschines 2.97.

3. Aeschines 1.38, 1.185 ("Against Timarchus").

4. Aeschines 1.130–131, 1.181, 2.127.

5. Aeschines 1.131.

6. Demosthenes 5.12 ("On the Peace").

7. Demosthenes 5.13.

CHAPTER 5. YOU HAVEN'T BEEN DEFEATED, FOR YOU HAVEN'T SO MUCH AS STIRRED

1. Harris, *Aeschines and Athenian Politics*, 110.

2. Philip Harding, "Demosthenes in the Underworld: A Chapter in the *Nachleben* of a *Rhētōr*," in Worthington, *Demosthenes: Statesman and Orator*, 266.

3. Demosthenes 6.21 ("Second Philippic").

4. Demosthenes 6.25.

5. Demosthenes 19.117 ("On the False Embassy").

6. Demosthenes 19.196–199.

7. Aeschines 2.154–156 ("On the False Embassy").

8. Demosthenes 8.61 ("On the Chersonese").

9. Demosthenes 8.50–51.

10. Demosthenes 8.60.

11. Demosthenes 9.27 ("Third Philippic").

12. Demosthenes 9.5.

13. Demosthenes 9.31.

14. Demosthenes 9.33.

15. Demosthenes 9.74.

CHAPTER 6. I ALONE DID NOT DESERT MY PLACE

1. Demosthenes 19.132–133 ("On the False Embassy").

2. Demosthenes 58.37–38 ("Against Theocrines"); Dinarchus 1.63 ("Against Demosthenes"); Plutarch, *Demosthenes* 14.4.

3. Plutarch, *Demosthenes* 14.

4. Plutarch, *Demosthenes* 13.

5. Plutarch, *Phocion* 23.

6. [Demosthenes] 12.1, 12.20 ("Philip").

7. [Demosthenes] 12.23.

8. Demosthenes 18.73 ("On the Crown").

9. Demosthenes 18.158–159.

10. Demosthenes 18.173.

11. Demosthenes 18.175.

12. Demosthenes 18.176.

13. Demosthenes 18.179.

14. Demosthenes 18.213.

15. Aeschines 3.154; Demosthenes 18.178.

16. Plutarch, *Demosthenes* 18.3; Hyperides, "Against Diondas," in Chris Carey et

al., "Fragments of Hypereides' *Against Diondas* from the Archimedes Palimpsest," *Zeitschrift für Papyrologie und Epigraphik* 165 (2008): 1–19.

17. Demosthenes 18.219–221.

18. Plutarch, *Marcellus* 21.2.

CHAPTER 7. DEMOSTHENES OF PAEANIA,
SON OF DEMOSTHENES, PROPOSES . . .

1. Athenaeus, *Deipnosophistae* 13.592.

2. Plutarch, *Demosthenes* 26.

3. Demosthenes 9.49 ("Third Philippic").

4. Aeschines 3.130 ("Against Ctesiphon").

5. Diodorus Siculus, *Library of History* 15.52.

6. Plutarch, *Phocion* 16.

7. Aeschines 3.150.

8. See Polyaenus, *Stratagems* 4.2.2.

9. Plutarch, *Demosthenes* 20.

10. Plutarch, *Moralia* 849a.

11. Demosthenes 18.249 ("On the Crown").

12. Demosthenes 60.18 ("Funeral Oration").

13. Demosthenes 60.22.

14. Demosthenes 60.24.

15. Demosthenes 60.26.

16. Isocrates, *Letters* 3.5 ("To Philip").

CHAPTER 8. HE ALWAYS SAYS AND DOES
WHAT IS BEST FOR THE DEMOS

1. Athenaeus, *Deipnosophistae* 2.22.

2. Plutarch, *Phocion* 21.

3. Aeschines 3.77 ("Against Ctesiphon").

4. Plutarch, *Demosthenes* 22.

5. Plutarch, *Phocion* 16.

6. Aeschines 3.160.

7. Diodorus Siculus, *Library of History* 17.15.

8. Plutarch, *Demosthenes* 23.

9. Hyperides, "Against Diondas" 1 (136v).

10. Hyperides, "Against Diondas" 2 (137v–136r).

11. Hyperides, "Against Diondas" 5 (176r–173v).

12. Aeschines 3.163.

13. Plutarch, *Demosthenes* 24; Dinarchus 1.35 ("Against Demosthenes").

CHAPTER 9. HE'S A GREEK-SPEAKING BARBARIAN!

1. Aeschines 3.132 ("Against Ctesiphon").

2. Aeschines 3.132.

3. Aeschines 3.133.

4. Aeschines 3.134–136.

5. Aeschines 3.166–167.

6. Aeschines 3.157.

7. Aeschines 3.153–156.

8. Aeschines 3.162, 3.174.

9. Aeschines, 3.172.

10. Aeschines 3.173

11. Aeschines 3.99.

12. Aeschines 3.216.

13. Aeschines 3.260.

14. Demosthenes 18.66, 67, 72 ("On the Crown").

15. Demosthenes 18.72.

16. Demosthenes 18.128.

17. Demosthenes 18.129–130.

18. Demosthenes 18.258–260.

19. Demosthenes 18.199.

20. Demosthenes 18.205.

21. Demosthenes 18.208.

22. Dionysius, "Demosthenes," 31; Demosthenes 18.209; Harvey Yunis, *Demosthenes: On the Crown* (Cambridge: Cambridge University Press, 2008), 227.

23. Demosthenes 18.256.

24. Demosthenes 18.258, 259–262.

25. Demosthenes 18.324.

CHAPTER 10. WILL YOU DARE SPEAK TO ME OF FRIENDSHIP?

1. Hyperides 5.31.b ("Against Demosthenes").

2. Dinarchus 1.84 ("Against Demosthenes").

3. Dinarchus 1.30.

4. Dinarchus 1.24.

5. Dinarchus 1.23.

6. Hyperides 5, fragment 5, columns 20–21 ("Against Demosthenes"), as reconstructed in Friedrich Blass's edition of Hyperides, *Hyperidis Orationes Sex cum Ceterarum Fragmentis* (Leipzig: Teubner, 1894).

7. Hyperides 5, fragment 5, column 21.

8. Hyperides 5, fragment 3, column 7.

CHAPTER 11. HIDE YOUR FACES FOR SHAME!

1. Demosthenes, *Letters* 3.37, 3.41 ("Concerning Lycurgus's Sons").

2. Demosthenes, *Letters* 3.41–43.

3. Demosthenes, *Letters* 3.44.

4. Demosthenes, *Letters* 2.20 ("Concerning His Own Return").

5. Demosthenes, *Letters* 2.2.

6. Demosthenes, *Letters* 2.5–6.

7. Demosthenes, *Letters* 2.7–8.

8. Demosthenes, *Letters* 2.13.

9. Demosthenes, *Letters* 2.20.

10. Demosthenes, *Letters* 2.26.

11. Plutarch, *Phocion* 22.

12. Demosthenes, *Letters* 1.2 ("On Political Harmony").

13. Demosthenes, *Letters* 1.6–8.

14. Demosthenes, *Letters* 1.10.

15. Demosthenes, *Letters* 1.12.

16. Demosthenes, *Letters* 1.13, 1.16.

17. Plutarch, *Demosthenes* 8.

18. Demosthenes, *Letters* 3.30.

19. Plutarch, *Demosthenes* 27.

CHAPTER 12. I DEPART FROM YOUR SHRINE STILL ALIVE

1. [Demosthenes] 59.33 ("Against Neaira").

2. [Demades], "On the Twelve Years" 51; Plutarch, *Phocion* 9.

3. Demosthenes, *Letters* 4.10 ("On the Slanders of Theramenes").

4. Demosthenes, *Letters* 6 ("To the Council and the Assembly").

5. Hyperides 6.20 ("Funeral Oration").

6. [Plutarch,] *Lives of the Ten Orators* 849b.

7. Plutarch, *Demosthenes* 29.

8. Plutarch, *Demosthenes* 30.

9. [Plutarch], *Lives of the Ten Orators* 846f.

10. Plutarch, *Demosthenes* 30.

EPILOGUE

1. [Plutarch,] *Lives of the Ten Orators* 851d.

2. [Plutarch,] *Lives of the Ten Orators* 847a; Plutarch, *Demosthenes* 30.

3. Plutarch, *Demosthenes* 31.

Bibliography

ANCIENT SOURCES

All references to speeches and letters in the endnotes use the numbering found in the standard collections of Demosthenes, Aeschines, Hyperides, and Dinarchus. These can be accessed online via the Perseus database or the web-based Loeb Classical Library, with the exception of Hyperides' "Against Diondas," for which bibliographical information is supplied. Plutarch's *Demosthenes* and *Phocion* are cited in the notes when they provide unique information or anecdotes that lack confirmation elsewhere. The *Lives of the Ten Orators* by Pseudo-Plutarch has been cited according to the Stephanus reference system.

Annotated versions of the speeches of all four orators are also available in print in the valuable series the Oratory of Classical Greece published by the University of Texas Press, series editor Michael Gagarin. The speeches cited in this volume are listed below.

Aeschines. Ed. and trans. Chris Carey. Austin: University of Texas Press, 2000.

Demosthenes, Speeches 1–17. Ed. and trans. J. Trevett. Austin: University of Texas Press, 2011.

Demosthenes, Speeches 18 and 19. Ed. and trans. Harvey Yunis. Austin: University of Texas Press, 2005.

Demosthenes, Speeches 27 and 28. Ed. and trans. D. M. MacDowell. Austin: University of Texas Press, 2004.

Demosthenes, Speeches 60 and 61, Prologues, Letters. Ed. and trans. Ian Worthington. Austin: University of Texas Press, 2006.

Dinarchus, Hyperides, and Lycurgus. Ed. and trans. Ian Worthington, Craig R. Cooper, and Edward M. Harris. Austin: University of Texas Press, 2001.

MODERN SOURCES

Buckler, John. *Aegean Greece in the Fourth Century BC.* Leiden: Brill, 2003.

Buckler, John, and Hans Beck. *Central Greece and the Politics of Power in the Fourth Century B.C.* Cambridge: Cambridge University Press, 2008.

Cawkwell, George. *Philip of Macedon.* London: Faber and Faber, 1978.

Bibliography

Ellis, J. R. *Philip II and Macedonian Imperialism*. London: Thames and Hudson, 1976.

Geiger, J., L. Ghilli, B. Mugelli, and C. Pecorella Longo, eds. *Plutarco. Vite Parallele: Demostene-Cicerone*. Milan: Rizzoli, 1995.

Hansen, Mogens H. *The Athenian Democracy in the Age of Demosthenes*. Norman: University of Oklahoma Press, 1999.

Harris, E. M. *Aeschines and Athenian Politics*. Oxford: Clarendon, 1995.

Lintott, Andrew, ed. and trans. *Plutarch: Demosthenes and Cicero*. Oxford: Oxford University Press, 2013.

MacDowell, Douglas M. *Demosthenes the Orator*. New York: Oxford University Press, 2009.

Sealey, Ralph. *Demosthenes and His Time: A Study in Defeat*. New York: Oxford University Press, 1993.

Worthington, Ian. *Demosthenes and the Fall of Classical Greece*. New York: Oxford University Press, 2013.

——. *Philip II of Macedonia*. New Haven: Yale University Press, 2008.

Worthington, Ian, ed. *Demosthenes: Statesman and Orator*. London: Routledge, 2000.

Index

Index

Aristion, 117

Aristippus of Cyrene, 157–158

Aristogiton, 144–145, 146

Aristophanes, 139

Aristotle, 65

Artaxerxes III (Great King), 12, 13, 24, 58, 68, 69, 76, 104. *See also* Persians and Persia

Artemisium, 123

Athenian Assembly: appeal from Amphipolis, 1–5, 31; appeal from Euboea, 38; appeal from Olynthus, 31–32; debate over Pagasae, 21–23; debate over Rhodes, 25–26; and the deification of Alexander, 131, 133; Demosthenes' address to regarding Thebes, 106–108; Demosthenes as envoy to Messene, 60; Demosthenes as orator, 10–12, 24, 26, 27–30, 61–63, 66–67, 80–81, 101; Demosthenes in, 1–2, 26, 27–30, 99; Demosthenes' letters to, 145–155; envoys to Philip, 44–45, 63; and the Exiles Decree, 130; inaction of, 30; peace treaty with Philip, 47–50; response to Philip's threat, 80–81; sends envoys to Greek states, 69; sends forces to Euboea, 38; sends forces to Olynthus, 40. *See also* Athens

Athens: alliance with Thebes, 81–84, 86, 89–91, 96, 97, 109, 150; and the Common Peace, 17–18; court system, 7–8; Demosthenes addressing, 32; and the Exiles Decree, 129–131; foreign policy decisions in, 57; funeral speeches, 95; Harpalus's money in, 132, 147, 152; Harpalus takes refuge in, 130; naval power of, 12–13, 15, 18, 24, 29, 77, 92; negotiations with Philip,

93–95; political power of, 17; prosperity of, 127–128; public funds in, 18, 28–29; and the revolt of Thebes, 105–106; Social War, 18; subject to Antipater, 161; Theban refugees in, 110, 115–116; and the Third Sacred War, 19–21; threatened by Macedon, 1–2, 4–5, 14–15, 22–23, 26–27, 31, 33, 58, 67, 88–89, 126; treaty with Philip, 47–50, 100–101; uneasy relationship with Thebes, 11, 12, 17, 33, 47, 55, 58, 59; war against Macedon, 78, 154–156; war with Sparta, 2–3, 4, 12, 17, 93. *See also* Athenian Assembly

Atrometus, 43, 120

Attalus, 104

Babylon, 128, 130, 147

Balkan tribes, 104–105

Boeotia: Alexander in, 82, 88; Athens's support for, 81, 84, 86, 89, 105; envoys to, 106, 107; loyal to Macedon, 154

Boeotian League, 83

Byzantium, 74, 76, 77

Calauria, 148, 150, 162, 163, 164

Callistratus of Aphidna, 6

Chaeronea: aftermath of battle, 100, 104, 108; Alexander at, 91, 103; Battle of, 90–93; Demosthenes at, 90, 92, 125, 150; Demosthenes blamed for 109, 110, 111, 116, 170; Demosthenes' defense of, 122–123, 125–126, 135, 149, 153, 156, 164, 169; eulogy for the dead, 95–97, 109; Philip's peace terms, 93–94; prisoners of war, 93

Chalcidice, 31–32, 33, 38, 41, 69

Chares, 21, 22, 33, 40

Index

Index

Index

Index

Index

Index